# END TO END

*Other books by Jonathan Thomas*

*Adventures in Anglotopia: The Makings of an Anglophile*
*Anglophile Vignettes: Fifty Little Stories About Britain*
*Anglotopia's Dictionary of British English*
*Visions of Anglotopia*

*Other Books by Anglotopia*

*101 London Travel Tips*
*101 Budget Britain Travel Tips*
*Great British Icons*
*Great Events in British History*
*Great Britons*

# End To End
Britain from Land's End to John o'Groats

By Jonathan Thomas

Copyright © 2023 by Jonathan Thomas

Cover Design by Jonathan Thomas
Cover Images by Jonathan Thomas
Cover Copyright © 2023 Anglotopia LLC

Anglotopia LLC supports the right to free expression and the value of copyright. The purpose of copyright is to encourage writers and artists to produce the creative works that enrich our culture.

The scanning, uploading, and distribution of this book without permission is a theft of the author's intellectual property. If you would like permission to use material from the book (other than for review purposes), please contact info@anglotopia.net. Thank you for your support of the author's rights.

Anglotopia Press - An Imprint of Anglotopia LLC
www.anglotopia.net

Printed in the United States of America

First US Edition: November 2023

Published by Anglotopia Press, an imprint of Anglotopia LLC. The Anglotopia Press Name and Logo is a trademark of Anglotopia LLC.

Print Book interior design by Jonathan Thomas, all fonts used with license.

All photographs © Jonathan Thomas

ISBN: 978-1-955273-28-2

# DEDICATION

*To Jackie, the best travel bestie a guy could ever hope for. The best part of this adventure was doing it with you.*

Note: Map is not to scale, locations approximate

# TABLE OF CONTENTS

Introduction..................................................................................1
A Very English Journey to Cornwall........................................15
The Polurrian Packet..................................................................21
A Place of Legend and Fantasy..................................................29
The Transatlantic Cable Museum..............................................41
Poldarkland.................................................................................49
Land's End: The First Tourist Trap?.........................................57
Every Seal Has a Name...............................................................63
The Minack Theatre....................................................................69
Cadgwith......................................................................................75
The RNLI.....................................................................................81
Doc Martin..................................................................................91
To Brisol.....................................................................................101
Castle Combe............................................................................107
A Meditation on Motorway Services......................................115
Hardwick Hall...........................................................................125
York.............................................................................................135
Ruined Abbeys...........................................................................147
The National Trust....................................................................157
Durham......................................................................................165
Barter Books..............................................................................173
Borders.......................................................................................181
Edinburgh..................................................................................189
The Royal Yacht Britannia......................................................197
Driving to Inverness.................................................................205
Loch Ness...................................................................................211
Dunrobin Castle........................................................................219
A Lament for Ackergill Castle.................................................231
John o'Groats.............................................................................239
The Queen Mum's House........................................................245
Scandinavians...........................................................................251
The Caledonian Sleeper...........................................................257
A Perfect Day in London.........................................................265
Epilogue: 1,392 Days Without Britain...................................273

# INTRODUCTION

When we departed for our epic drive across Britain from Land's End in Cornwall to John o'Groats in Scotland in 2018, I did not know that it would be the last time I was able to visit Britain for four years. I wish I had. I would have savored every minute of that trip just a little bit more. I would have paused more to take in the landscapes. I would have spent longer at the castles and ruins we explored. I would have enjoyed every bite of British cuisine just a little bit more. I would have crammed four years of travel experiences back into those two weeks we spent driving from one end of Britain to another.

The idea of taking a drive from Land's End to John o'Groats was something I'd wanted to do as long as I knew it was something that people did. It was firmly at the top of my

Britain bucket list. But it was something we knew would be hard to manage - it would take a couple of weeks to do it properly. That meant it would be expensive, and it also meant we'd have to take a lot of time away from our kids and responsibilities at home. We generally tried to keep our journeys to Britain around a week, at most 10 days, as that was the most our young children could stand us being gone (and the most we could stand being away from them and, let's be frank, probably the most our trusted caretakers could stand to care for them!).

I'd filed away doing 'LeJog' into the things we would do far in the future, maybe once the kids were older. LeJog is the official shorthand acronym for travelling from Land's End to John o'Groats.

But then, of course, I was inspired.

Inspiration comes in many forms. Mine came from YouTube.

Two prominent YouTubers ran a major Kickstarter campaign to raise funds to do the nerdiest thing you could possibly imagine: travel to every train station in Britain (there are more than 2,500 of them). Run by a man obsessed with Britain's trains, it was a journey that would take them almost three months. One of them took a sabbatical from work to do the trip. Not only did they raise all the funds they needed to do the journey - and crucially cover the costs of producing dozens of YouTube videos about it - they raised more than their goal, which meant they could make even more videos and then a proper documentary about the journey when it was done.

I thought the whole thing was brilliant (in the British sense).

I love Britain's trains, so I was thrilled to watch their journey. But there was something more - I connected with the couple on a personal level. They were of a similar age to my wife Jackie and me. They were very much in love with each other, as Jackie and I are. When the male of the couple did interviews about their trip - it was all over the headlines at the time because it was so WEIRD, and the British press loves weird - he kept saying the same quote over and over.

It was from Ernest Hemingway - one of my personal favorite writers (yes, there are things I love that aren't British - shocking revelation, I know). The quote was "never go on trips with anyone you do not love." And I thought that was a lovely sentiment. Even before we started our publication Anglotopia, Jackie and I traveled around Britain, and those travels were a crucial part of our love story. So many of our most wonderful experiences as a couple were during our travels around Britain.

So, what better way to repeat that than to peel away from our kids for two whole weeks and drive from one end of a history-filled country to another?

An idle conversation about doing something similar led to excited conversations about actually doing something similar. The sales pitch was simple. We could drive from Land's End to John o'Groats and take our time and do it properly. Think of the material we could get for the website and magazine (at the time, we ran a print magazine). Think of the experiences. Think of two whole weeks going from nice hotel to nice hotel, just us. Just us alone and in our love. Just us on an adventure.

Wouldn't that be great?

We put it on the calendar for September 2018.

But first, let's explore the history of travel around Britain, and then we'll begin our own journey from Land's End to John o'Groats.

\*\*\*

Before Britons conquered one-quarter of the world, they first had to get to know their own island. Even as recently as a few hundred years ago, parts of Britain were so remote they might as well have been in Antarctica. People lived there, but they were people who barely considered themselves part of Great Britain. London was as far away mentally as Paris or Rome or Istanbul (if they even knew what those were). And I'm not talking about the remote people's not knowing anything about Great Britain; I'm talking about everyone else on the island. Life was restricted in Britain until the railways were built. You lived and died within a few miles of where you were born (and to be fair, most people to this day still do that). The first great explorers in British history didn't just set off to explore the oceans of Earth; they set off to explore the island of Great Britain itself. In some cases, no one had ever really thought to do such a thing!

As someone obsessed with Britain, I'm a bit obsessed with reading books or watching TV shows about people who've journeyed around Britain. It also turns out that Brits themselves love to read about their own country - especially when it's written by an acceptable outsider (American Bill Bryson is one of the few). Britain's literary heroes and other historical figures have a long history of journeying around their island and seeing what's there. Instead of visiting a foreign country, they'd visit Scotland, which was just as foreign as anywhere else in Britain.

For most of Britain's history, people didn't get around much. There was no such thing as tourism. Traveling was dangerous, and it was only done when necessary or under great protection. People didn't wake up one day, have an existential crisis about the struggles of current work/life balance, and go on a journey to a distant county. No, traveling around Britain just wasn't done. While the Romans left Britain a decent road network, which was improved upon, the roads were often a muddy, dangerous mess.

In some cases, it was quicker to sail on a boat to get around Britain!

For millennia, people have wondered just what was on the island of Great Britain. It even piqued the interest of Caesar, who invaded and colonized it . When William the Conqueror took control of England in 1066, the first thing he did was commission an inventory of his new kingdom (now known as the Domesday Book) to find out what was there. For many places in Britain, this was the first time their names were recorded in written history. Even today, it's a mark of pride for villages and towns in England if they're mentioned in the Domesday Book.

In pre-Norman days, the only people traveling around on anything other than 'official' business would be monks. They were the first real tourists. While they had the mission to spread religion everywhere they went, they often found themselves in far-flung lands that most people would never find themselves in. And as they were usually the only literate people around, they were the first to write down their experiences.

It's not like they were keeping a blog of their travels, though.

Monks like the Venerable Bede or William of Malmesbury were some of Britain's first proper historians, and their books are a guide to life long past. They vividly describe places simply to describe them (and give their Christian importance.). William of Malmesbury is fascinating - he was a polymath born in Wiltshire. His great works were Gesta Regum Anglorum (Deeds of the English Kings) and Gesta Pontificum Anglorum (Deeds of the English Bishops) - the former a guide to English kings until that point around 1100 and the latter a guide to famous English bishops. But it's his writing about places that is most interesting.

He said this about Shaftesbury, my favorite English town:

> "Shaftesbury is only a town, though once it was a city. It is situated on a steep hill. Evidence of its antiquity is given by a stone in the chapter house of the nunnery. It was transferred there from the remains of the ancient wall and reads, 'King Alfred built this town in 880, in the eighth year of his reign.'"

You have to admire his crisp, clear writing. What's most remarkable is that you could describe Shaftesbury like that today, and it would be exactly the same.

The next traveling monk worth mentioning is Gerald of Wales. He lived a positively international jet-set life - making several journeys all the way to Rome. Having demonstrated his usefulness to King Henry II, Gerald was selected to accompany the Archbishop of Canterbury, Baldwin of Forde, on a tour of Wales in 1188. The goal of the trip was to recruit soldiers for the Third Crusade, but it's his account of that journey, the Itinerarium Cambriae (1191) and the Descriptio Cambriae in 119, which are the most long-lasting legacy of that trip.

On his journey during 1188 he completed a circuit around the whole edge of Wales, from beginning to end. His description of Barry Island, near Cardiff, and famous as the home of Stacey from the hit British rom-com Gavin and Stacey is positively delightful:

> "Not far from Caerdyf is a small island situated near the shore of the Severn, called Barri, from St. Baroc who

formerly lived there and whose remains are deposited in a chapel overgrown with ivy, having been transferred to a coffin. From hence a noble family of the maritime parts of South Wales, who owned this island and the adjoining estates, received the name of de Barri. It is remarkable that, in a rock near the entrance of the island, there is a small cavity, to which, if the ear is applied, a noise is heard like that of smiths at work, the blowing of bellows, strokes of hammers, grinding of tools, and roaring of furnaces; and it might easily be imagined that such noises, which are continued at the ebb and flow of the tides, were occasioned by the influx of the sea under the cavities of the rocks."

Nothing nicer has been said about Cardiff since! I jest, I jest. I can't find any evidence of Gerald finding any evidence of any temporal anomalies or sexy Americans trying to save the universe.

We have to fast forward a few centuries to find another notable traveler around Britain, John Leyland (or Leland). Leyland was not a monk but was educated and lived life rather like he was one - and his life was intertwined with the convulsions of Reformation Britain. He was a poet and is considered the father of English local history and bibliography. Many of the techniques he laid out are still used to this day when trying to write of the local history of places in Britain - he established the 'county' as the basic unit to study local history in England, which is still done today.

After the Dissolution of the Monasteries, Leland dedicated his life to hunting down important books, and that took him on journeys around most of Britain. Along the way, he took meticulous notes on what he saw, heard, and did. We call this Itinerary, and when a new edition was published in the early 20th century, it ran to five volumes!

Here's an example of what he said about Fowey in Cornwall:

> "Cornwall, there stands a poor fishing village called Bodennek. There is the passage or trajectus to Fowey. Miles above Bodennek into the land northward is a creek upon the north side, there is a sect monks of Montegu, and is dedicat to S. Sirice and Juliet."

But as Britain developed as a society and civilization, the blogging monk trend ended in the Middle Ages, as non-clergy began to make their way around Britain and write down what they saw. And women too. Celia Fiennes explored England on horseback, journeying the entire length and breadth of the country just to travel for its own sake. It was unheard of for men to do this, and even more, unheard of for a woman to do it, often alone. Why did she travel? She said it was to "regain my health by variety and change of air and exercise." It doesn't sound much different from those who seek to travel to find themselves these days!

Fiennes worked up her notes into a travel memoir in 1702, which she never intended to be published. She wrote them for her family. Thankfully, they thought differently because her writings provide a vivid portrait of a still largely unenclosed English countryside with few and primitive roads. Extracts were published in 1812, and the first complete edition appeared in 1888 under the title Through England on a Side Saddle. Since then, her writings have never gone out of print.

Celia had various interests, including anything new and shiny in technologies. She particularly liked England's bustling towns; such as the newly fashionable spa towns such as Bath and Harrogate, and capitalist commerce. Fiennes saw many of the finest baroque English country houses while they were still under construction. You may not realize that many stately homes have always been somewhat open to travelers; it's not a new pastime for Brits. Her comments are among the most interesting sources of information about them. At Stonehenge, she counted the exact number of stones, and at Harrogate visited "the sulfur or stinking spaw." She even clambered over the rocks at Land's End, just like we did. It's fascinating to be connecting with the history of fellow writers who have made the same journeys and same discoveries - that Britain is such a fascinating and varied place, with a beautiful landscape worth seeing for its own sake. I'm glad I'm not alone in this!

By far, the most well-known journey around Britain, however, is the one undertaken by Daniel Defoe. Yes, the author of Robinson Crusoe was an adventurer himself. His account of his various travels through the island of Great Britain became his bestselling work - and best known for Brits – while we know him best for Robinson Crusoe. The book was not a raw travelogue, but rather it was a compilation of a lifetime of travel around Britain. Defoe had a varied life. He was famous as a political pamphleteer and is often called the father of modern journalism. He was born as Daniel Foe in 1660, the son of a butcher in Stoke Newington in London, but used the grander sounding 'Defoe' as his pen name. He was arrested, pilloried, and imprisoned in 1703 for a pamphlet he wrote satirizing high church Tories. But it's his accounts of Britain that have stood the test of time.

He also visited Land's End and had this to say: "I am now at my journey's end; As to the islands of Scilly, which lye beyond the Land's End, I shall say something of them presently: I must now return sur mes pas, as the French call it; tho' not literally so, for I shall not come back the same way I went; but as I have coasted the south shore to the Land's End, I shall come back by the north coast, and my observations in my return will furnish very well materials for a fourth letter."

Traveling around Britain started to become more common after this. It really took off when a chap named Thomas Cook had the idea to sell excursions on Britain's newfangled railways. They proved insanely popular, and Thomas Cook, the Travel Agency, was born (and it survived well into the $20^{th}$ century, though it did not survive poor management, sadly). The advent of the railways led to an explosion of wandering around it. Traveling around Britain was no longer solely the preserve of the wealthy or the educated. Anyone who could afford to go on a train could get the experience. And it was with this that we see the birth of Britain's tourist industry and the advent of the first tourist traps and attractions. Many of the railways went to the seaside and deposited travelers there.

As Britain's railways developed and the road network was improved, it was no longer the rule for people to live and die where they were born. They could visit cities. They could visit special places like romantic ruins and castles. They could visit the seaside. They discovered an island of wonder all around them. They discovered the island we know of today as travelers around Britain. I'm sure they were just as excited as we are to learn what a wonderful place they lived in.

During the $20^{th}$ century writers like H.V. Morton started writing about Britain with affection, taking a detailed look at the land they lived in. His works, like In Search of England, are must-reads for any Anglophile. And, of course, one mustn't forget Bill Bryson, the American who wrote Notes from a Small Island. In that book, Bryson was preparing to return to

America and set out on a journey all over Britain. It's one of the biggest-selling books about Britain ever written (its sequel is equally as good).

I only hope that my own scribblings can one day add to the canon of writers who've written about Britain. *Waves hello to the historian who managed to find an out-of-print copy of this book in an old library for his research.

# ROUTE PLANNING

Planning this drive ourselves proved a challenge. One of the problems we ran into is that no one has actually written a guidebook about driving "LeJog," the official shorthand acronym for Land's End to John o'Groats. There are books about walking it. There are books about cycling it. I bought all of them but, if you're planning to drive, they're not much help. I also wanted to plan our route to take in a few things I've always wanted to see along the way - so we wouldn't necessarily be following the traditional routes people take for LeJog. Most routes plan it using the shortest possible route; I had other ideas.

So, planning was me with a big map on the dining room table with a pencil, circling things I'd always wanted to see, roughly following the LeJog route that The Great British Adventure Map recommends, but altering it when there was something I wanted to make sure we'd visit. We gave ourselves two weeks to make this journey. Good friends of ours offered to 'show us' Cornwall and that leg, so that would take three full days (plus the drive down from Heathrow, but I'm getting ahead of myself).

To an American, an 800-mile drive doesn't sound that interesting. By American standards, an 800-mile car trip is a sneeze. It is not a long distance. You can do it in a day. Many people do LeJog in a day. But that 800 miles in Britain is different. Britain has a continent's worth of landscapes in the space of 800 miles. If you do it in a day, you would miss out out so much. Even the television series Top Gear made the journey in a day. But a day is not enough and would not be enough for us.

After careful research, we decided on two weeks for the whole trip. The rough outline would be the first few days in Cornwall with our friends (they would fetch us from the airport and drive us down to Cornwall), then drive north to Bristol and pick up our own rental car, then from there hit the Cotswolds, then drive to Yorkshire. Then on from there to Northumbria. Then Edinburgh. Then north through Scotland, with two more stops, finishing in John o'Groats and then taking the Caledonian Sleeper train from Inverness back to London (with one final day in London). It would be a whirlwind.

That was not the traditional LeJog route, but it would be OUR route, and that's all it needed to be. We planned the trip to visit places we'd never been before. By this point, I'd been to Britain almost 20 times, and there was still so much of the country that I hadn't seen. This is something that people commenting on our website or our social media channels love to point out (you only ever go to Dorset or London, blah blah). We simply needed to explore new places. It would give us years of content worth writing about and years of pictures to share (when we planned this trip, I didn't plan to write a book about it - that came much later).

The entire trip was the biggest, most ambitious thing we did for Anglotopia up to that point. We'd see so many important sites, travel through many important landscapes, and FINALLY visit Scotland, something I'd wanted to do my entire life. This book is not a guidebook to the trip; it's about our journey and the places we encountered along the way (as an aside, there still isn't a good guidebook for driving LeJog, I suppose I should write one after this!).

In the weeks before the trip, I finalized our route and our hotels and stops for the night. When we tallied up the entire route, we'd be traveling well over 1,000 miles. We'd start at Heathrow. Drive southwest to Cornwall, then north from Cornwall up the spine of Britain, all the way to the tip top (well, not tip top - we didn't go to Dunnet Head). We'd start at the Thames, continue to the English Channel, and end with the North Sea winds blowing in our faces.

# CHAPTER ONE
## A Very English Journey To Cornwall

It's a long drive from London Heathrow to Cornwall. But it's the best drive. Cornwall is a long way from everywhere, especially when you've had a nine-hour flight. The first part of our drive would be a bit odd because we wouldn't be doing any driving at all. Instead, our very good friends would be driving. As we'd never been to Cornwall and their family had a holiday cottage they planned to visit anyway, they offered to drive us to Cornwall and show us around. We'd pick up our car later in Bristol and continue on our way.

This was going to be a nice treat, as now I would not have to drive for five hours right after getting off a transatlantic flight.

This journey was old hat to our friends, so they were well prepared for a long journey. The car was fully fueled, they were packed, and they brought along a cooler with plenty of food and snacks for the drive. This was a pleasant surprise as we were starving, and they kept us well-fed and watered the entire journey. We like to joke that they're our surrogate English family, and it was like going down to Cornwall for a holiday with our parents.

When you travel to a place enough, you make friends. Sometimes deliberately, sometimes accidentally. We once rented a cottage in Shaftesbury, Dorset, for a stay on Gold Hill to fulfill a dream. The owners stopped by to meet us and wish us well. They stayed for hours as we chatted. Then we got together again for tea and chatted for hours. A friendship was born out of a strange set of transatlantic circumstances. Eventually, we visited their home and became friends. On more than one occasion, they've driven us around to see THEIR England.

We've shared countless cups of tea. And it's a good reminder that in my 20 years of travel around Britain, the most rewarding thing we've gotten out of it isn't seeing a bunch of pretty places or having a ton of fun experiences. It's making good, lifelong friends. It's one of the best unintended consequences of running the business that I do. It's a strange universe where you become good enough friends with somebody that they volunteer to drive you for five hours to Cornwall, then show you around for a few days.

I highly recommend you all get some good British friends. You won't regret it.

Making British friends enriches your travels around Britain so much - and gives you more reasons to come back, so you can hug them again. Chat with them again. Experience the joys of life with them again. It's been over 1,000 days since this trip, I miss England every day, but I miss seeing our friends most of all.

It brings a smile to my face to think back to that day in September 2018, when our friends were waiting for us at the arrivals gate at Heathrow, just like in the film Love Actually, holding hot cups of tea for us.

The first part of the journey to Cornwall isn't that interesting, as you're just driving through suburban London but then, once you hit, say, Hampshire, the roads thin out, and you begin to see beautiful green countryside all around you. And we would be seeing a lot of it on that trip.

For many British people going to Cornwall was their first major holiday, especially for older generations, as going to Cornwall was equivalent to going abroad. It was as close to aboard as you could get in the days before cheap package holidays to Europe. And Cornwall was magical for the English because it was so far away. It was also a foreign place. They spoke their own strange version of English. It was filled with moody tales of smugglers, storms, and foggy moors. But there was also golden sunshine that in the summer seemed to last forever in the long hours of summer English sunlight. Windswept beaches filled with people. People swimming in the cold North Atlantic (some in wetsuits because the water is COLD). Tea and coffee in beachside cafés. A vibe of relaxation. Cornwall is a fantasy.

And I was very excited to finally see it for myself.

There's something elemental and a bit of a shared cultural experience around a long car trip to a far-distant destination. Cornwall was the holiday destination for Brits, the same way that Americans would go to Disneyland or drive along Route 66. Where the long journey to get there is a part of the going as the actual experiences that you have when you reach your actual destination. No one remembers the thrills of the roller coaster; they remember wiling away long hours on the road - in some cases, extremely bored (or bickering with a sibling).

I'm happy to report that nobody fell asleep on our journey down to Cornwall! We always have great conversations with our English friends, plus the ample food and, eventually, cups of tea. It was a massive fun drive down, and I'm so glad that we didn't do it by ourselves, jet-lagged, or take the overnight Cornish Riviera sleeper train.

All along the way to Cornwall there are landmarks that people recollect that are more remembered for the anticipation of getting to them than the actuality of seeing them. It's much like when you drive from Chicago to Atlanta and you see the signs for Ruby Falls or Rock City. The one time you actually stop to see these tourist traps, inevitably, you end up disappointed. Yet you don't regret stopping. The journey to Cornwall has similar experiences. There's a brief view of Stonehenge. There's the mystical Jamaica Inn, made famous by Daphne du Maurier in the novel of the same name (of course, we stopped briefly, enough for me to get a picture).

The most rewarding aspect of this journey to Cornwall was that it felt like we were kids, going on a holiday to the seaside. Everything was a new experience. We had no idea what to expect when we got to Cornwall. We just knew it would be nice. As a student of British culture, I'm hungry for the type of experiences that British people have in their lives. Christmas. Half-term. Guy Fawkes Night. Experiencing these things helps me have a greater understanding of them and helps fulfill that fleeting wish that I'd grown up in Britain but didn't.

I never had these experiences growing up, but our

English friends who drove us to Cornwall did their best to give us an approximation of the experience of the anticipation of driving there for a holiday experience at the seaside, and I couldn't help but feel nostalgia for a childhood I never had. Thinking back on it now, four years later, it almost pains me to tears from the nostalgic joy of those times. But that wouldn't be a stiff upper lip, then, would it? But I think of this drive often, and I'm filled with warmth remembering our English friends telling us about their memories of their childhood journeys to Cornwall and how things have changed a lot and how much of it hadn't changed. Some things are universal.

It was the perfect way to begin our grand adventure.

# CHAPTER TWO
## THE POLURRIAN PACKET

I don't know if I've said this before, but the roads in Britain are not straight. There are straight roads, sure - the straightest ones were built by the Romans and still exist. But the default shape of the roads in Britain is not straight. They follow the contours of the ever-changing landscape. Up and down. Left and right. Down and up. Right and left. Endless bends.

The motorways of Britain do their best to get rid of a lot of these quirks and variations through the sheer will of blasting through the landscape. But when you get off the motorways and dual carriageways (a divided highway) and onto smaller country roads, you are presented with a very different kind of driving. You're not even guaranteed to have two lanes on every road.

And the roads will never, ever be straight.

My wife and I come from the Midwest. Most of the Midwest was laid out in a tidy little grid when it was first surveyed after the American Revolution. And that grid turned into a grid of roads. It being a largely flat and easy-to-navigate landscape, most of our roads are straight. They go in either of two directions, north and south, or east and west. British roads, being hundreds of years older and following a landscape that is almost never flat, can go north, south, east, and west on the SAME ROAD.

Once we left the motorway somewhere in the West Country, the final leg of our journey to Cornwall was on country lanes that would test the stomachs of two people who'd just arrived in England off a transatlantic flight and were both tired and hungry.

After stopping for some fresh air and brief pictures when we arrived at the Cornish coast and saw the sea for the first time, we headed for our hotel. When we planned the trip, our criteria for the hotel was simple: we wanted to be in a hotel on the sea. Not hard to do in a county surrounded by sea on three sides.

The Polurrian on the Lizard was recommended to us by our hosts and would be our base for the next three nights. The hotel is a luxurious retreat nestled on the rugged coast of Cornwall. With breathtaking views of the Atlantic Ocean, this historic hotel has been a favorite of travelers for over a century. Originally built in 1900 as a private residence, the Polurrian was converted into a hotel in the 1920s and has been a beloved destination for discerning travelers ever since.

The hotel's stunning location on the Lizard Peninsula offers guests a unique opportunity to explore the wild and beautiful Cornish coastline. From the hotel's gardens, guests can enjoy panoramic views of the sea and the rugged cliffs, while the nearby beaches offer opportunities for swimming, surfing, and sunbathing.

Inside, the Polurrian on the Lizard is just as impressive. The hotel's elegant rooms and suites are furnished with antique furniture and modern amenities, providing guests with a comfortable and luxurious stay. Over the years, the Polurrian has played host to many famous guests, including Winston Churchill, who stayed at the hotel during World War II.

When we arrived at the hotel, we were almost too tired to notice the surroundings. But when we entered our hotel room (which was rather sparse but nice), the first thing we did was look out the window. We had a sea view. We opened it immediately and could hear the waves crashing against the cliffs below, we immediately caught a chill breeze, which was refreshing. We had some time to settle in and rest before leaving for dinner with our hosts later.

And it's at this point in the trip that I made a discovery that would change our lives and our business, just a little bit at least. We desperately needed a cup of tea to perk us up. We needed to stay awake until the evening, or else the jet lag would win. We needed a nice strong cuppa. Most hotels in England will provide you with everything you need to make a cuppa.

Most will offer a local tea.

The Polurrian offered a tea we'd never had before: Cornish Tea. Its teabags ae orange, with a stark black logo. It was the only tea option on offer. So, we boiled the kettle and made some tea while we unpacked and listened to the ocean outside. Once the tea was cool enough to drink, my eyes went wide, and I looked at Jackie.

"This tea is amazing," I said, taking another sip.

"Yes, it is," she concurred, taking her own sip.

"It's smooth and delicious and refreshing."

Tea loyalty is a strong thing with Brits, and with this particular Anglophile. My favorite tea at that point was Yorkshire tea (and it's still my morning drink).

"I'm in love," I said. Jackie rolled her eyes.

For the rest of our time in Cornwall, the only tea on offer pretty much everywhere in Cornwall was this Cornish Tea. I drank it at every opportunity. I bought a box and was sure to bring it home. It became my after-lunch tea of choice. Then I ran out, but I was already addicted. I needed more of it!

After some research, it appeared that no one sold Cornish Tea in the USA. HOW WOULD I GET MORE?!?!?!

Well, I did what any other self-respecting owner of a business that already imported British products to the USA would do. I contacted them and wondered if they would wholesale to us and ship to the USA. They were delighted to, as long as we were willing to pay the high shipping costs and import duties and deal with all the paperwork.

Within days, I had dozens of boxes of Cornish Tea. I listed it for sale on our online store and sold out practically within a day. It turns out there was a great demand for Cornish tea in the USA! We've now been stocking it for almost five years, and it's always a brisk seller.

And I always have a ready personal supply of Cornish Tea because this business owner always saves a few boxes for himself.

I'm getting ahead of myself.

Back to Cornwall.

Another thing we discovered was the concept of non-refrigerated milk. Most hotels will give you room temperature, shelf-stable milk to put in your tea. It's not that different from the creamers we have in the USA, except it's actual milk. It's called UHT milk, or ultra-high-processed milk. The milk goes through extra processing that completely sterilizes it and makes it shelf-stable for months. Every hotel in Britain will have these on offer. While nothing beats fresh milk, it's good enough.

Some Brits will sneer at the UHT milk as not good enough to put in tea.

When we mentioned that unusual milk to our hosts, they told us what they do when traveling.

"We put a creamer full of milk in the sink in the bathroom with some ice," he said.

A very British solution to a British problem, real milk for your tea while traveling.

As we enjoyed our tea, a piece of paper was slipped under the door. On it, it said The Polurrian Packet, and it appeared to be the hotel's own newsletter. It featured interesting history about the hotel, but it also showed current beach conditions, and the weather forecast. It was a delightful little thing, and I applaud that hotel employee who probably had the thankless task of putting it together.

It also introduced me to a word I'd never heard before. Under the weather conditions, it said it would be a bit 'mizzly.'

Curious, I asked our hosts later what that meant, and basically, it means it's rainy, but not pouring, and the drops are small. It's cloudy, and you basically feel like you're walking through a cloud. Apparently, it's like this a lot in Cornwall (yet it's a Scottish word). On the day we arrived, it was definitely a bit mizzly. But one thing you learn about Cornwall is that, while it could be mizzly at any given time, the sun could also shine at any time. The weather in Cornwall is beautiful and prone to change based on the moods of the Atlantic Ocean.

After our rest and refreshments, it was time for dinner.

But that meant getting back on the twisty, turny roads again. This time, we were heading for one of the oldest estates in Cornwall, Trelowarren, home to the Vyvyan Family, who've lived there for nearly 600 years. At the time, the 'Lord' of the estate was a young 18-year-old who liked pizza, so he installed a brick pizza oven in an old barn. He'd created a lovely little ad-hoc pizzeria in the middle of the Cornish countryside. The pizza was delicious, and the surroundings of a crumbling romantic Cornish estate were right out of Poldark (more on that later). As of the third edit of this book, a new couple runs the café, but they still serve fresh pizzas.

    The weather in Cornwall was cool that night, and the wood-burning fire at the pizza place was very welcome. It kept us warm for our first Cornish twilight, but it was also a sign of things to come - the weather was going to be colder than we planned, and there was going to be a storm. Still, there's not quite anything more pleasurable than enjoying good artisan pizza on a crumbling English estate with good friends by the fire.

*Jonathan Thomas*

# CHAPTER THREE
## A Place of Legend and Fantasy

Deep in the mists of time, legend has it that the island that St Michael's Mounts sits upon was constructed by a giant named Cormoran. Cormoran was allegedly 18 feet tall, and he supposedly took massive blocks of granite from the mainland and used them to construct the island and his lair (along with his giantess of a wife). He lorded over the island as his own domain but treated the mainland as his hunting ground. He was a nuisance to the locals. He would steal their cattle, their chickens, and sometimes their children, to satisfy his almost unquenchable appetite.

Eventually, they had enough.

A farmer's boy named Jack decided to do something about it (in some versions of the story, the local council asks him to do it). He comes up with a cunning plan to trap the giant. He digs a big hole in the ground and hides it. Then with the confidence we should all have before we do an impossible task, he blows a horn to summon the giant from his lair. As Cormoran comes after Jack, presumably thinking he looks like a tasty snack, in his haste, he does not notice the hidden hole and then falls to his death as the tide rolls in to doom him to a salty, watery grave. On the stairs that take you up to the castle today, there is a heart-shaped rock that is claimed to be the giant's heart, forever encased in the stone of the place.

It's a grand story and the type of beguiling tale that makes English legends live in the popular American imagination. I remember reading a few years ago that the bones of a very large man, said to be 10 feet tall, were once found in the dungeons of St Michael's Mount. As with many legends, perhaps there was an element of truth.

It was stories like this that attracted me to St Michael's Mount. I'd read about the place for years. It's one of the most photographed places in Britain. A granite hunk sitting in a beautiful Cornish bay. It's a place that is easy to photograph and make look beautiful even in the gloom that surrounds it most of the year.

When we planned this drive, I knew we had to finally make a point to visit this special place. It was the first thing I wrote down when we were deciding on our Cornwall itinerary.

It's always quite something to see a place you've dreamed of for years with your own eyes. We'd set out early with our hosts so that we could cram in as much as we could that day. The Mount was to be our first stop. Even with an early start, Marazion, the town where the Mount is connected, was almost an hour away. We had a pretty but gloomy drive along the coastal road. And without even realizing how close we were to it, the island appeared in view as we rounded a bend.

Our driver helpfully stopped at a convenient pull-off (or lay-by as they are called in Britain) so that I could take pictures. I was there, finally. We drove on down into Marazion and parked in the car park. It was a cold and blustery September day. The tide was in, so there would be no walking to the mount today, we would have to take a boat. The weather was turning, and an Atlantic storm was due to hit the next day. You could feel Cornwall bracing for it in the air. One got the feeling that the whole town was battening down the hatches.

I'd never been on the sea before. In 20 trips to the UK, I've only ever flown over the ocean, I've never been on it. The only boats I've been on have been on small lakes and on the Chicago River in the American Midwest. It's not that I was afraid of it or worried about seasickness. I just never had the chance. I finally had the opportunity to go out on the sea. And it was lovely.

The signs in Marazion direct you down to the seafront, where a stone weir recedes into the bay. When the tide is low, you can take a leisurely walk across the bay along a cobbled path. That morning, the tide was high, and the bay was very choppy due to that incoming storm. The island hadn't been closed yet. We watched as the first boat came across the bay, it appeared slowly, and then it was right in front of us. The boatmen helped everyone on board, and we paid our fare (it was £2, I believe, per person).

And with that, I was on a boat, on the sea. Well, if you count Mount's Bay as being the sea. Immediately it was like being on a roller coaster. The boatmen turned the boat around and pushed the throttle to its maximum, and we began the crossing. Thankfully the boat was covered; otherwise, we would have been soaked as the boat smacked into the waves as it crossed. Up and down. The noise was so loud we could barely hear ourselves talk. Up and down. Up and down. Left and right. We occasionally smacked our bodies into the side of the boat. No one was brave enough to stand except the boatmen, whose legs were steady as tree trunks. Thankfully, I have a strong stomach and didn't get seasick.

The crossing took only ten minutes. It was rough, but fun. Halfway across, I mentioned to Jackie that this was the first time I'd been on the sea, and she was surprised – even after almost 20 years together, we still managed to surprise each other. It wasn't long until the water began to soften as we entered the sheltered harbor on St Michael's Mount. The boat softly touched the harbor wall, and we all claimed off. My legs were surprisingly steady. The crossing over had been exhilarating. But it was time for a cup of tea.

On one hand, we had to stop for tea because the castle wasn't yet open, so we needed to kill a little bit of time. On the other hand, stopping for tea is something we always make an effort to do when we're traveling across Britain. Why? Because it's how the British see their country. They divide their day when out and about by when they can have a cup of tea. Tea punctuates the day as a refreshment. It's an opportunity to stop and enjoy the company you're with. To get a caffeine injection. To talk about what you're doing. To enjoy your surroundings. And, most important of all, to have a piece of cake.

The entire economy of Britain is arranged in a way for British people to be able to get a cup of tea. You can get one ANYWHERE. I don't mean there are Starbucks everywhere (because, of course there are). No, most places people spend more than a little bit of time in will have a place to get a cup of tea. You'll find tea in the strangest places. A great British pastime is visiting the local garden center. It's not just a place where you buy some plants and landscaping materials. It's a place you can spend the day at. There's a shop. There are restrooms. There's a café or restaurant. The quality of the tea is VERY important. If it's bad or too expensive, the business will fail! I've even been in an antique store in an old warehouse in Dorchester, and guess what they had in the place? A small café to get a cuppa.

When we're back home in the Midwest, and we're planning to be out for the day, I now plan my day around when I can have my morning and afternoon cuppa (if I don't, I'll want to take a nap!). I always make note of where we can get tea nearby, but as America has something to learn about serving proper tea, I often bring my own tea with me. In the back of my car, I have a small woodfired kettle and everything needed to make a cup of tea, in a pinch. Once, I was in a store, and found the most British invention ever: a car tea kettle. The store owner made clear they sell a lot of them.

There is nothing more sublime and pleasurable than sitting in a busy National Trust café and enjoying a hot cup of tea and a piece of cake or a brownie. They're almost always busy and filled with the noise of people enjoying their day out and the clinking of teacups, whistling of kettles, and the clang of cutlery. Some of my happiest memories of our travels across Britain are while we were resting for a cuppa. It's an especially nice respite when it's raining outside or particularly cold. Sometimes, we'll stop at an attraction just to have a nice cup of tea even if the place is closed for the season (but the café is still open).

The St Michael's Mount café was just opening, but happy enough to serve tea and cake. We sat outside and watched the choppy waters of the bay we'd just crossed. We were protected from the harsh winds by the solid rock island behind us. But there was a buzz in the air of the approaching storm. It was chillier than we'd expected so the warm tea was a welcome respite as we looked at the long climb we would have to get up to the castle. Tea was fortitude.

Once time had passed the massive wooden gates to the path up to the castle were opened, and it was time to make our climb.

St Michael's Mount is genuinely stunning in reality. You don't really get an idea of its scale from pictures of the place. Standing on the harbor wall, you look up, and the castle is a distant climb up a massive hill. The island is bigger than you expected, and the castle is up higher than you imagined. Then you realize you have to walk all the way to the top of that hill to get to the castle. Tea was definitely required first.

A former medieval monastery that is now a sprawling castle set atop an offshore island seems very much like the setting of a fairy tale. But the tumultuous Middle Ages, Henry VIII's dissolution of the monasteries, and more contemporary British crises such as World War II, have made St Michael's Mount an important historical stronghold, scenic but strategic. Today, St Michael's Mount offers visitors a picturesque castle, well preserved but also much altered over the centuries, and elegant sub-tropical gardens with a pretty harbor below.

There is evidence that St Michael's Mount was inhabited at least as early as the Neolithic era (circa 4000-2500 BCE). It may have been used as a trading port for continental merchants picking up Cornish tin bound for the Mediterranean during the first few centuries AD. According to Christian legend, St Michael appears on the rocks on the mount in 495 AD to warn local fishermen of the dangerous local stones. This connection to a saint would help turn the mount into a pilgrimage site.

Edward the Confessor gave the Mount to the Norman abbey of Mont Saint-Michel, another famous island village in France, almost directly across the sea. Benedictine monks from this abbey were invited to establish a priory in Cornwall, an invitation they accepted and, over the next few centuries, carefully and painstakingly built their church.

In 1425, the monks also laid a rough causeway that, at ebb tide, makes the mount accessible on foot from the landward side. The monks lived in peace for a number of years until St Michael's Mount became a strategic base for Perkin Warbeck, a pretender to the throne of King Henry VII. After Warbeck's failed rebellion during the War of the Roses, he sought refuge in St Michael's Mount.

Following King Henry VIII's Dissolution of the Monasteries (1536-1540), St Michael's Mount was occupied by a number of crown-approved military governors who kept the fortified island in good shape and defended it against Parliamentarian forces who tried to take it in 1642 during the English Civil Wars. Their victory was short-lived as St Michael's Mount was surrendered to Parliamentarian forces in 1646 and fell under the command of John St Aubyn, a Parliamentary colonel who was nominated governor and began to adapt the existing building on the mount, part monastery, part castle, into a residence. The family still live in the castle to this day. Descendants of John St Aubyn, the Lords St Levan, live at St Michael's Mount and are responsible for the many architectural transformations the building has undergone.

Some parts of the medieval incarnation of St Michael's Mount remain, such as the gatehouse, the converted Lady Chapel, and the church and refectory with garrison quarters underneath. The church is thought to date back to the 13th century, and St Michael's chapel to the 15th. What was initially the monastic refectory, built in the 12$^{th}$ century, became the Tudor Great Hall and features a magnificent arch-braced roof. This roof was restored in the 19th century, at which point the room entered the third stage of its existence and became known as the Chevy Chase Room. This name comes from the incredible plaster friezes of hunting scenes that line its walls. A Jacobean oak table with a full set of monastic chairs completes the imposing effect.

The most revered room at St Michael's Mount is the old monastic Lady Chapel, which was converted into a glorious drawing room during the mid-18th century. With views from the north terrace of the very summit of the island, this carefully conserved Georgian treat has interiors in the style of Strawberry Hill Gothic, featuring pretty, pale blue and white ornamentation and a significant landscape of the mount itself by artist John Opie.

The rest of the castle displays the old barracks and museum rooms. Several other buildings can be found dotted around the castle, including a row of late 19th-century houses known as Elizabeth Terrace, some of which are occupied by castle employees. You will also find the former stables, laundry, steward's house, and two former inns.

But to see all of this, we would first have to climb the Pilgrim's steps to get to the castle. After our refreshing tea and cake break, we began the trek up the hill. We took our time, it would take a while, and it was steep. This notoriously out-of-shape American would have to take it easy. It did not help that the cobbles were wet and slippery.

We slowly made our way up the hill, following in the footsteps of pilgrims in the days of old who came here to visit the shrine of St Michael. As we climbed, we got closer and closer to the castle, and its immense size became much clearer. The path up the hill follows a curve as it brings you around to the other side of the island. Up close, the castle very much looked like it was a much a part of the island and the very rock it sat on. It didn't look built on the rock, it looked like it was the rock, carved from it. When we finally reached the top, we were exposed to the sea and the wind straight off the Atlantic Ocean, which we had not experienced on the other side of the island.

The wind was blustery, and at the very edge of the ramparts, we struggled a bit to stand up straight against the wind. A storm was definitely coming. And the island was bracing for it as it has done for centuries. The castle entrance was covered in scaffolding, a common sight for places as old as this which require constant maintenance. We made our way into the castle and out of the wind.

It was immediately much quieter. The stone of the old castle walls shut out the oncoming storm outside. It was crazy to think that even when the storm really got going, you would probably barely notice it within these thick stone walls.

The castle is not a grand house by any means. Thankfully it wasn't crowded that day, because if there had been just a few more people it would have been difficult to get around. There are few grand rooms in the castle, at least open to the public. The Chevy Chase room was probably the 'grandest' room. It's very clear as you wander around that this was a castle and has always been a castle and a very functional military installation until it was made into some kind of home for the lords of the island.

The island was given to the National Trust in the 20th century, but the St Aubyn family worked out an advantageous deal with the Trust where they could continue to lease the castle (and live in it) while continuing to run the business side of the island. So, you have this strange experience of visiting a National Trust property that's also a private enterprise. The experience is slightly different than you would get at most other

Trust properties - such as a lack of NT branding throughout the place. The family still lives here, and the current Lord lives in his castle, even if it is no longer technically his.

We made our way through the rooms in the castle and then found ourselves outside again, even higher up than we were before. The wind was getting stronger. All the video I shot at this stage was useless because of the sound of the wind. We found the highest point on the island, which is itself embedded in the castle wall, proving that the castle is more a part of the mountain than a separate structure. You're supposed to touch the spot and make a wish. Jackie and I dutifully did so (our wish is our secret!).

The chapel was probably my favorite part of the Mount. A lovely little atmospheric place. They had choral music playing inside from a speaker, and it really set the mood. We stayed for a minute to take in the place. I'm not religious, but I always find the peace of these places fulfilling in my own way.

Before we knew it, we'd seen all the castle had to offer and it was time to head back down the hill. We overheard one of the guides saying that they would be closing soon to shut the castle and prepare for the arrival of the storm. We'd visited just in time. Soon, the island would be cut off from the mainland for a few days. Lord St Aubyn's island would return to his lonely care, as the island stood silent sentry against whatever the storm sent his way.

What a romantic thought.

Though he would probably stand in his great hall, watching the waves lashing his famous garden below, and worry about the fall in admissions and how that would affect his annual revenue.

Still, I would happily trade places with him.

I did not look back at the Mount as we drove away from

Marazion. I fell under the spell of the place, and I knew that I would have to return. Maybe that time to take a walk on the ancient path that leads from the mainland to the island.

# CHAPTER FOUR
## The Transatlantic Cable Museum

This stop on our trip was one of those that serendipity led us to. Of course, I was aware of Cornwall's history in transatlantic communications. When Jackie realized that we were so close to an entire museum dedicated to it (her career in communications made this an interest, and she was actually writing a paper on the topic for her master's degree at the time), we knew we were going to have to stop, despite our tight schedule. It was the mid-point of the day, and we were already a bit tired after exploring St Michael's Mount (and taking two boat rides). A sedate museum would be nice. And we only had to pop in.

Because Cornwall is at the very far southwestern edge of England, it is also the closest connection to the rest of the world, and it has been since the first transatlantic telegraph cable was laid during the Victorian era. Before this cable was laid down on the Atlantic Ocean floor, it would take weeks for a message to get from North America to Britain. It would take months from India or Australia. The world was disconnected from itself, which is something that's very difficult to imagine now. We rely on communications cables to connect us, and it all started with the first transatlantic cable coming from Porthcurno, Cornwall, in 1870.

We like to think of the Internet as a 'new' thing created in our lifetimes. But in truth, the Victorians created the first Internet - first with telegraph networks spread out over Britain, Europe, and North America, and then globally when the first undersea cables were put down at great danger and great expense.

We take for granted how easy it is to communicate with one another. No matter where we are in the world, we can pick up a phone and call, text, or email someone on the other side of the planet. Of course, this wasn't always the case, and the world got a lot smaller when the first transatlantic cables were laid out connecting Europe and North America. Despite the advent of wireless and satellite communications, the fundamental bedrock of global communications is still piped under the ground and under the sea.

For years the village of Porthcurno was a simple fishing and farming haven on the tail end of the English mainland. Its name comes from the 16th century Cornish spelling "Porth Cornowe" which originated in the Cornish language as "porth cornow." This name was a reference to the nearby rock formations and meant "cove/landing place of the horns/pinnacles." While it had some limited activity for fishing and as a port, the destiny of Porthcurno changed forever with the coming of the first transatlantic cable. From the late 19th century onwards, the village would be associated with transcontinental communications. It was, quite literally, the center of global communications (and still is to some extent).

The earliest attempt to link up wired communications came in 1857, courtesy of the British and American governments. Two ships, the HMS Agamemnon and the USS Niagara, laid 2,500 miles of cable from Ballycarbery Castle in County Kerry in Ireland to Newfoundland, Canada but, during several attempts throughout 1857 and 1858, the cables repeatedly broke, and the effort was abandoned. Another attempt with the ship Great Eastern in 1866 proved successful and finally connected the British Isles with North America. The accomplishment emboldened the United States, Canada, and the United Kingdom to try again, this time in the village of Porthcurno.

In 1870 the village became home to the first transcontinental submarine telegraph cable to reach India from the United Kingdom. In the past any message from this distant part of the British Empire to London took about 40 days. Britain attempted to construct a cable in 1864 that went underwater as well as above ground, but the land portions suffered from attacks by local residents, necessitating the Porthcurno cable that was entirely underwater. The Falmouth, Gibraltar, and Malta Telegraph Company was formed in 1869 to create the new line. As the name might suggest, Porthcurno was not their first thought for the telegraph station, but a late-stage switch was made after it was determined that ships' anchors in Falmouth posed too great a risk.

The laying of the cable was overseen by John Pender, a Scottish cotton merchant who had been part of the 1858 attempt by the Atlantic Telegraph Company. By 1872, Pender's Falmouth, Gibraltar, and Malta Telegraph Company merged with at least two other telegraph companies responsible for laying the London-India Telegraph Line to form the Eastern Telegraph Company. The Eastern Telegraph Company would go on to be a powerhouse in wired communications, laying lines all over the globe in what some historians now refer to as the "Victorian Internet."

At the center of all these worldwide communications was the village of Porthcurno and its small telegraph operations station, established in 1872, with PK as its code name. It had just 16 young men operating it, who were often described as badly-behaved and ill-disciplined. However, as the Eastern Telegraph Company grew, so did the Porthcurno Telegraph Station. In 1904 the station moved to a new building called Eastern House and in 1909 the new station expanded for the first time with a building to house equipment, while the 1904 station building served as offices and accommodation for the staff. By 1920, the station was the largest in the world, with 14 cables that had their terminus in Porthcurno.

The importance of PK Porthcurno to the British Empire was never more apparent than during World War I and World War II when the Ministry of Defence invested a great deal of resources in its protection. The First World War saw 43 soldiers stationed at Porthcurno to guard the station, and that number was increased to 300 at the start of the Second World War in 1939. Gas-proof doors were also installed, as well as numerous pillbox fortifications along the coast. And that's not even the tip of the changes as the area around the station became heavily fortified with artillery, and permits were required to come anywhere close to the building.

By 1929 the British Government had merged all the telegraph companies into one entity, Imperial and International Communications Ltd, which became Cable & Wireless Ltd in

1932. By 1950 Porthcurno wasn't just a center for sending cable messages, but it was a major training center as well. Cable &Wireless established the C&W Engineering School here in 1950, where students completed part of their eighteen-month-long course to become engineers. Eventually, the entire course was moved to Porthcurno and would remain here until 1993, when the school was moved to Coventry, and the old building was torn down.

Unfortunately, as other technologies were on the rise, telegraph cables became a thing of the past in Porthcurno. The last cable was laid between Porthcurno and Newfoundland in 1952. The station itself was then closed in 1970 as the last telegraph connection was removed from service. Then the aforementioned school moved in 1993, removing the last active connection the village had with the communications industry. However, all was not lost, as much of the Eastern House remained as a testament to Porthcurno's importance to British history. What remains of Eastern House was converted to the PK Porthcurno Telegraph Museum in 1997, and the building was designated as a Grade II listed building in 2008.

Today the PK Porthcurno Telegraph Museum stands as a legacy of an important era in worldwide communications. It was started by C&W employees and passionate volunteers who worked to preserve a number of documents and artifacts related to the station's 100-year history. Its exhibits not only include the history of the station but also the surrounding village and the World War II tunnels meant to protect the facility. The museum also puts on talks, science workshops, and more.

And this is where we enter the scene, stopping off on our epic journey to Scotland to have a look at the history of global communications. We had an hour, which we ended up concluding wasn't really enough time to do the museum justice.

We wandered around the exhibits - the coolest thing was seeing and being able to touch a piece of former transatlantic cable (and crucially seeing a cross-section of what it actually looks like - it's not a simple thing!). There were ongoing group tours, a gift shop, and a café.

But my favorite bit was outside the main building and in a tunnel on the hill behind the museum. This was the 'secret' part of the museum where you could see working examples of telegraphy - and the actual rooms where the cables came up from the ocean. Handy displays explain how everything works, and it's truly a marvel to see it in action - and it makes you realize how brilliant those early pioneers really were. There was also ample information on the role of the place during the World Wars. My favorite part, though, had to be the sound of all the restored equipment, typing and clanging away like it was still the hub of global communications.

PK Porthcurno stands as a testament to what has come before in uniting our world and how cable telegraphs helped pave the way for the wireless communications on which we rely today. Cornwall still plays an important geographical role in global communications. Several transatlantic fiber optic cables - the modern grandchild of those early copper cables - still come ashore in Cornwall - bringing the global Internet to Britain (and out of it). Their actual location, however, is secret because why would it not be?

*Jonathan Thomas*

# CHAPTER FIVE

## Poldarkland

During our trip, there was one British TV show that was at its height of popularity. A Georgian-set drama full of adventure and derring-do with plenty of romance, dramatic landscapes, and heaving bosoms. That show, of course, was Poldark, which is ever present when you visit Cornwall. Every gift shop has some kind of Poldark related merchandise, some official, some not-so-official. Even at a tiny little artisan gift shop at the end of the Lizard Peninsula, you could find a mug with Ross Poldark's face on it. As fans of the show, we knew we'd have to incorporate it into the trip somehow.

Cornwall is the land of Poldark. The landscape is as entwined in the stories as the characters we know and love. And those stories go back much further than the 2015 BBC series lets on. The Poldark book series, which is a set of 12 historical novels, was written by Winston Graham and published between

1945 and 2002.

Graham was a prolific British author, but is best known for his Poldark series of books. He was not Cornish by birth but was actually born in Manchester in 1908. However, he was raised in Cornwall and drew inspiration for his books from the rugged landscape and rich history of the area. He began his writing career as a journalist and went on to publish over 40 novels, including several acclaimed standalone works. Graham's writing was known for its vivid descriptions and complex characters, and his work has been adapted for stage, screen, and television.

The Poldark books tell the story of the Poldark family and their struggles in Cornwall, England, during the late 18th and early 19th centuries. The first book in the series, Ross Poldark, was published in 1945 and introduced us to the main character. Ross Poldark returns to Cornwall after fighting in the American Revolutionary War and finds that his father has died and his estate is in shambles. He sets out to restore his family's fortunes but faces many challenges along the way.

The second book, Demelza, introduces us to Ross's new wife, Demelza, a former servant girl he marries after falling in love with her. The rest of the series follows the ups and downs of their marriage, as well as the lives of their children and other members of the Poldark family in the intervening years. It's a generational story with issues that many families today would identify with.

The books were incredibly popular when they were first published, and they have remained so ever since. They have been adapted for television twice, first in the 1970s and again in 2015 (more on these later).

One of the reasons for the success of the Poldark books was their vivid portrayal of Cornish life during the late

18th and early 19th centuries. Graham's descriptions of the landscape, the people, and the social and political issues of the time are incredibly detailed and immersive. The books are also notable for their strong female characters, such as Ross's wife Demelza, and his cousin Verity.

Most Americans became familiar with the show (and the series of books) when the classic Poldark TV series was first adapted for television in the 1970s, starring Robin Ellis as Ross Poldark. The series ran for two seasons and 29 episodes; it was a huge success, with millions of viewers tuning in each week when it aired on Masterpiece Theatre (and in a poll in 2007 was voted the best British drama ever). The show helped to popularize the Poldark books and cemented the character of Ross Poldark in the public consciousness in both Britain and America.

But that was a long time ago and, in entertainment terms, might as well have been 100 years ago. By 2015, Poldark was ripe for a new adaptation, filmed with the latest HD technology and cameras that could show off Cornwall in a way that simply was not possible in the 1970s with limited BBC budgets. Of course, Masterpiece came on board as co-producers. It was low-hanging fruit as far as entertainment goes.

In 2015 the new adaptation, starring Aidan Turner as Ross Poldark, premiered on both sides of the pond. The series was an instant critical and commercial success and was praised for its beautiful cinematography, strong performances, and faithful adaptation of the source material. Viewers were particularly taken with Aidan Turner's abs, which became world famous from the promo photos (and one could argue this show made Aidan Turner more well-known than his appearances in the Hobbit films). The series ran for five seasons and 43 episodes, ending in 2019.

The new adaptation was particularly popular with younger audiences, who were drawn to the show's blend of romance, drama, and historical detail. It has also helped to bring the Poldark books to a new generation of readers, many of whom have been inspired to delve deeper into the history of Cornwall and the social and political issues of the time.

So, while we were in Cornwall, the show was at its zenith of popularity and you could absolutely tell. Between Poldark and Doc Martin, Cornwall was probably the most well-known place in Britain to Americans, outside of London. We talked to our hosts about all of this, and they knew the perfect place to take us, and it just happened to be on our route on our way to Land's End: Porthgwarra.

Porthgwarra is a small coastal village located near the southern tip of Cornwall. The village is famous for its stunning beaches, rugged cliffs, and picturesque landscape. It is a popular tourist destination, attracting thousands of visitors every year who come to enjoy the beautiful scenery and explore the rich history of the area. It's also colloquially known at the 'Poldark Cove,' as the picturesque place was used as a location several times.

The history of Porthgwarra dates back to the 18th century when it was a thriving fishing village. Viewers of Poldark would know that village was known for its abundant supply of pilchards, which were caught and exported all over Europe (and were a key plot line in the show). The pilchard industry was the mainstay of the local economy, and the village grew rapidly as more and more people came to settle in the area. In Poldark's era, the pilchard harvest was a communal activity, with everyone banding together to spot and then catch the abundant fish. If the harvest was a failure, it would be a tough winter for the residents.

Then in the 19th century, Porthgwarra became an important center for the mining industry. The village was situated close to several important mines, and many of the local people found employment in them. The mining industry brought significant wealth to the area, and the village prospered, helping to stabilize the economy from relying just on pilchards.

But these days, both the pilchards and the mining industry are long gone. Now, Porthgwarrais is a popular tourist destination.

We arrived at Porthgwarra, and we could immediately see its appeal as a place to visit and as a shooting location for a big budget BBC drama. The place is remote, the village is small. It is quiet in a way that only a place six hours from London could be. Because of the time of year, there weren't many people about, so it had a quiet, alluring atmosphere. When you hike to the cove, you're presented with the most beautiful emerald-blue water. Beyond the cove is the edge of the English Channel where it turns into the vast Atlantic Ocean.

The cove was an incredible sight to see and instantly recognizable from the TV show. It still feels very much frozen in time, as there are old wooden boats chained up on the beach, ready to go out to sea and go fishing (how often they still do, I don't know). An ancient winch stands sentry at the top of the cove, waiting to haul the boats up from the water into the safety of the cove for storage. Jackie loved the cove and ran down to the edge of the water barefoot to dip her toes into the ocean.

"It's freezing!" she shouted back over the roar of the waves hitting the cliff sides around us.

It was a glorious sight.

Porthgwarra is a unique and fascinating place with a rich history and a strong connection to the surrounding landscape. It is a remarkable place, and interestingly, the cove is privately owned, which is unusual these days (the public is welcome to visit and enjoy it, however). Visiting made me want to settle into the couch and binge watch the entire series of Poldark all over again.

Poldark offers us a glimpse into a world that is very different from our own, and yet the themes of love, loss, and family are timeless. It's both familiar and alien at the same time. The stories will be endlessly popular, as all good stories never really fade away. Standing in Porthgwarra, with the wind blowing around you, and the gorgeous sea crashing into the cliffs ahead of you, you can't help but feel you're in a dramatic scene. If you squint, you can almost see Ross Poldark on horseback on the cliffs above.

I can say I've walked in the footsteps of Ross Poldark (well, of Aidan Turner), and it was very rewarding. Though, I'm afraid I don't have the abs to match.

*Jonathan Thomas*

**LAND'S END 2018**

NEW YORK 3147

JOHN O'GROATS 874

ISLES OF SCILLY 28
LONGSHIPS LIGHTHOUSE 1½

ANGLOTOPIA
17TH SEPTEMBER

# CHAPTER SIX
## Land's End: The First Tourist Trap?

Land's End has a romantic-sounding name. But it's basically an amusement park now. And it actually isn't the furthest western point in the British Isles, that's down a lane and accessible without a fee. Land's End just has the branding.

We generally avoid tourist traps on our travels; Britain has so many heritage attractions worth seeing, so why waste time in tourist traps at all? London Dungeon? No thanks. Yorvik Viking Centre? Pass. Alton Towers? No thanks, we have theme parks at home. But the very nature of our journey from Land's End to John o'Groats necessitated a visit to one the most famous tourist traps in the world, Land's End.

We'd already spent a day or two in Cornwall, and technically our drive would not actually begin until we visited the famous sign and had our picture taken to prove that we'd been to Land's End. As John o'Groats purports to be the northernmost part of Great Britain (it is not), Land's End is in some ways its counterpart and where all the 'End to End' journeys either begin or end.

This part of Cornwall is so appropriately named for being the very tip of England and its westernmost point. Also known as Peal's Point, Land's End is a headland, a narrow piece of land that projects from mainland Britain. From here, it's an 874-mile journey to John o'Groats, the other 'end' of Britain.

As with most things in Britain, it has a history that stretches back further than written records or human memory. Archaeological discoveries have unearthed artifacts from as long ago as the Mesolithic Period (10,000 to 4,000 BC) in the area. The Ancient Greeks called the area "Belerion," which means "The Shining Land." The first recorded name in modern times was "Penwith Steort" in 997, penwith being Cornish for "extreme end" and steort meaning "tail or end." By the 14th century the Middle English name for Land's End was "Londeseynde," and by 1500 the Cornish name was "Penn al Wlas" or "End of the Land," from which its present name derives.

Its modern status as a tourist locale seems to have begun in the 17th century with poet John Taylor visiting the area hoping to find subscribers for his new book. By the Victorian era at least 100 peoplecould be found at the landmark at any given time. A small home at Carn Kez would look after horses for visitors who wanted to walk the cliffs and, over time, that house eventually grew into the present-day Land's End Hotel.

A Cornish family owned the land on which Land's End sits until 1982, when they sold it to Welsh real estate magnate David Goldstone who tried to develop the 105-acre site, but ran into resistance from the locals after he instituted an admission charge in 1983 (it is still free to visit Land's End). Goldstone then sold Land's End in 1987 to Peter de Savary, who developed much of the current attraction, including a small theme park. In 1989, de Savary also purchased John o'Groats for £2 million, becoming the first person to own both famous ends of Great Britain. The current owners purchased the property in 1996 and formed Heritage Great Britain PLC to manage it.

While certainly a very real place, Land's End also has its share of mystery and myth. It's said that giants and faeries once roamed the land before men. Cornwall is often regarded as one of the areas of Britain where King Arthur's legendary kingdom of Camelot was located. One Land's End legend known as The Lost Land of Lyonesse says that there was a country named Lyonesse that was part of Arthur's kingdom that was lost to the waves when it fell into the sea. Cornish fishermen have sworn for centuries to have seen the spires of the lost country under the sea, and some believe that the Isles of Scilly could be the mountaintops of that former land.

Land's End obviously revels in these legends. They're a currency they use to extract as much from visitors as possible. When we arrived it was not crowded, and we walked right through the main thoroughfare that leads to the actual Land's End sign. The air is filled with the smell of fresh fried donuts and chips. There are plenty of overpriced places to eat, nestled next to souvenir shops and, bizarrely, some well-known British High Street names.

Modern Land's End offers many attractions that tie into its history, legends, and the land that inspired them all. The place is basically an amusement park now. While seeing Land's End is free, there are plenty of paid attractions. Arthur's Quest gives children of all ages a chance to enter Arthurian legend, while the Aardman Experience is where you can interact with some of their most famous settings and characters, such as Morph, Shaun the Sheep, and Wallace and Gromit. There's also the Jolly Roger 4D film experience and Greeb Farm, where you can interact with the animals. Plenty of climbers visit Land's End each year to tackle the cliff faces, while others are content to walk around and take in the view as the Victorians did before them.

  We gave all of these things a hard pass. We just wanted to see the sign and, to be fair, it was easy to avoid paying for anything extra, so I applaud the owners there. However, you do have to pay for the car park, which is offensive to the English people's sense of thriftiness. Though the donuts did smell delicious, and I was tempted by the Aardman Experience. I am, sometimes, at heart, a bit of a tourist.

  We arrived at the sign. There was not much wind that day, the skies were blue, and the sun shone brilliantly on the sea beyond. It was quite something to finally see the edge of England, jagged cliffs standing stately against the onslaught of the Atlantic Ocean. All that stands between you and North America is the endless blue sea.

  It's quite something to see in person.

  Of course, we had to get our picture taken at the sign. The sign attraction is a family affair. There's a small area where a team of people take pictures of tourists for a few pounds a shot. For a little extra, they will send you on a print of the picture. They were very kind when we told them we were on an adventure and filming the process; they were happy to use our camera and take some pictures for us. We made sure to spend as much as we could as a thank you. We had our picture, filmed a short video for our vlogs, and went on our way.

  Our 874-mile journey to Scotland had officially begun. We were in and out in under an hour, with our wallets intact. It was rather exciting to have finally done something I've always wanted to do.

I still wish I'd gotten the hot donuts, though.

We didn't get much of a sense of a beginning of our journey by visiting Land's End. Yes, we ticked the box, visited the sign, and got the postcard. But we'd already traveled several hundred miles by road from London and had been exploring Cornwall already. Really, it felt like an interlude. But still, we did it. The journey 'started.' Even if we weren't properly driving just yet.

# CHAPTER SEVEN
## Every Seal Has a Name

I was excited about Lizard Point because of the donuts. Or rather, the prospect of having a second breakfast that consisted of a giant donut, as sold to me by our driver. The breakfast at our hotel was... not good. And it was by far the worst part of our stay in Cornwall. So, while we ate it dutifully, I was looking forward to a hot and delicious donut by the sea.

Lizard Point is the southernmost point in Britain. Next stop, France. You can't go further south than this on the British mainland, so it seemed fitting to visit this place on a drive taking us from the bottom of Britain to the top.

The selling point of Lizard Point, beyond the promised views, was the little café there, right at the edge, that served hardy British fare.

And donuts.

As much as I love Britain's coastal landscapes, really,

the donut was enough to sell me on visiting there.

When we pulled into the car park, I was hungry for a second breakfast. But first, I was awe-struck by the views. To the south was an endless sea. If you drew a straight line south, the nearest land would be Spain (though if you drew a slightly crooked line to the east, the nearest land would be Britany in France). If you drew a straight line to the west, it would be thousands of miles long before it hit Newfoundland. If you think about it, it's truly one of Britain's places furthest away from anything other than Britain. Such remoteness is alluring.

Especially to seals, but I'll get to that.

First, donuts.

The Wave Crest Café is perched on a cliff overlooking the sea. Below it is a small shelter where volunteers watch the birds and the seals that live in the water. Directly to the east is a lighthouse, which has been warning ships away from the rocky shores of Cornwall since 1752. There used to be a lifeboat station here, and if you follow an old slipway from the Wave Crest down to the sea, you can have a look at it. It's no longer a RNLI lifeboat station, and locals use the slip to launch small boats. The station is a ruin, a relic of another time, permanently there simply because it was built of such sturdy stuff that it's impossible to remove.

We took a table in the café, overlooking the sea. The sea was angry that day. I've never spent much time at the seaside, and I'd never really experienced it like this. Lake Michigan, my home body of water, does not get waves like those I saw in Cornwall that day. It was a marvel to watch the sea churn around the rocks. It's amazing how the rocks don't budge or fall over. Wave after wave. If you looked closely, you could see a gray figure bobbing up and down in the surf. It was not human. It was not a rock. It was alive.

It was a seal!

If you looked closely, you would see another and another.

And that's why retired old men were crowded around the National Trust hut - they were there to keep an eye on the local seal population.

"All the seals have a name, you know," our driver said. "Each one has a personality, and each one has its own name."

What a bizarre notion, I thought. Not only that men would sit here all day, sometimes every day, watching out for bulbous and entertaining seals. But that they would be able to tell them apart enough for each of them to have a name. What life do these wayward seals get up to, I wonder?

The sun was shining, despite the impending storm rolling in, upsetting the sea. It glistened off the violent surf like a million diamonds. Outside there was a constant din of the waves crashing on themselves and on the rocky coast . A relentless movement that never stops and has never stopped as long as Britain has been separated from the European mainland.

It's definitely the most remarkable place where I've eaten a donut.

Which was very good, by the way. We had our donuts. Enjoyed a hot cup of tea in the warmth of the Wave Crest Café. And watched the storm come in, and the seals bob up and down in the water.

I don't know their names. But it's comforting to know that even years later, as I write this, the same seals are searching for fish in the coves around Lizard Point, and there's a chap there in a windbreaker coat with a pair of binoculars saying, "Yep, there's Nigel again." And noting it down studiously in a log.

I wonder how many storms there have been since?

I wonder if they still have the donuts?

*Jonathan Thomas*

*Jonathan Thomas*

# CHAPTER EIGHT
## The Minack Theatre

Throughout Britain, there are amazing places that have no reason to exist. They could not be built now. No one would be insane enough to attempt it, and no local planning council in their right mind would grant planning permission (what the British call building permits). The Georgians and Victorians built follies on the grounds of their stately homes, many of which still stand. A chap built a replica of an Italian village on the coast in gloomy Wales (Portmeirion). People have built stately homes to look like fairy-tale castles or have turned fairy-tale castles into stately homes (see later chapter on Dunrobin Castle). Or they begin a world-class opera festival in their back garden in the middle of a war (Glyndebourne). Or they build a world-class theater on the side of a cliff overlooking the ocean.

As I said, it's mad.

And the woman to do such a mad thing was the formidable Rowena Cade, who built a theatre on a cliff, often with her own two hands, in her own back garden.

Like the Odeons of ancient Greece, whose stone seats climbed up hillsides and provided some of the earliest entertainment in the Western world, the Minack Theater in Cornwall is a similarly styled entertainment venue, though one that's a bit more modern. Minack is intriguing, at least for appearing so ancient when it's actually less than 100 years old (the name Minack derives from the Cornish word "meynek," which means "rocky place" - a fitting name for the very rocky area). At the beginning of the 20$^{th}$ century, this spot was simply a rocky slope overlooking the Celtic Sea. One woman thought that it looked like a natural amphitheater. So, she decided to build one. The destiny of this small part of the Cornish coast was fated to change with the arrival of one Rowena Cade after the First World War.

Rowena Cade was born in Spondon, close to Derby, in 1893 and moved to the area with her mother following World War I. She purchased the Minack Headland for just £100 (nearly £6,600 in today's money - still a great deal for coastal real estate!) and built her home overlooking the sea. Shortly afterward, in 1929, Rowena became involved with a local theater troop for its performance of William Shakespeare's A Midsummer Night's Dream. The group then put out the word that they were looking for a place to perform their version of The Tempest, and Rowena decided to turn the cliffs below her garden into their new stage.

Rowena had absolutely no experience in gardening or landscape design but, with the help of her gardener Billy Rawlings, they worked to clear the granite boulders and earth from the cliffs and transform it into an entertainment venue with a terrace and seating down the cliff to the stage itself. When the Minack Theater opened in 1932 for the performance of The Tempest, it enjoyed a beautiful and dramatic setting with the sea as its backdrop, very much in keeping with the play itself. The performance even got a mention in The Times newspaper. Whereas the theater enjoys a very professional technical setup today, this wasn't the case for its first performance. Cade helped make the costumes herself, and the lighting was provided with batteries and car headlights.

It was a very British make-do and mend affair!

Such was the success of that first performance that Rowena Cade dedicated herself to improving the theater. She often worked on it during the winter months between performance seasons for the remainder of her life. Working with her gardeners, they added grass to the seats and built some of the earliest structures for the players as well as adding a simple trestle table from which to sell tickets. Over the years more was added to the Minack Theater to turn it into the professional performance venue it is today.

The coming of the Second World War halted Minack's stage performances, and the Army took over the spot to serve as a lookout position. There was a gun post built into the theater during WWII. After the war, the gun post was converted into a ticket office as part of the theater's restoration. Before the war was over, it was used as a setting in the 1944 film Love Story starring Stewart Granger and Margaret Lockwood. After the war, Cade and her gardeners worked on restoring the theater back to what it had been and adding some additional features, including a road, a car park, and a flight of steps leading up from the beach. By the time Rowena died in 1983, she had left behind an amazing legacy in UK theater by creating one of the most unique venues in the entire country.

Of course, that is not where the story ends.

And this is where we enter the story. When I knew we would be in the area, I was determined to stop and have a look. It was the theatre's off-season, so we could not see a performance (and frankly, we didn't have time). But when there are no performances scheduled, the place is open for tourists to have a look around and gawk at the views. When you're walking from the car park there's no indication that there is something special beyond the squat buildings housing a gift shop and ticket office.

It's only once you pay your small admission fee (which goes to funding the theatre's operations), enter through a set of doors, and then walk through a small garden that you round a bend and are presented with a view that you will not find anywhere else on this planet. An aqua-blue North Atlantic Ocean lashing against the cliffs below. But inexplicably, there is a theatre with quite a few seats clinging for dear life to the edge of Britain. The wind was fierce that day because of that approaching storm I keep mentioning, but it was truly one of the most remarkable places I'd ever been. All carved out of the cliff by a determined woman and her gardener.

The drop is precipitous down to the sea, and you have to remind yourself that you're very safe. You could not trip and fall into the rocks below. There are plenty of railings and setbacks to prevent you from meeting a Cornish fate. It's hard to imagine being perched up here on a cold summer evening, with the wind lashing against you as you try and watch a play. I bet it's both incredible and terrifying.

When you find out that the Minack Theater puts on some 20 performances each summer season and sees over 150,000 visitors annually, you simply don't believe it. HOW?!?!? While the theater was originally built for Shakespearean plays, all manner of comedies, dramas, pantos, and everything in between are put on there. Today the Minack Theater includes larger facilities, such as a balcony looking over the theater for those with accessibility needs, professional level lighting and sound, and a café and gift shop. Visitors can also take a tour of the gardens that Rowena Cade helped to cultivate, and the gift shop even includes cuttings from the garden that you can take home and add to your own backyard. The Minack puts on performances from Easter through September and reopens briefly during December for Christmas-related programming (that has to be quite cold!).

It's a testament to the English landscape, which has been shaped for centuries by eccentrics like Rowena Cade. The ruins of their ambitions are everywhere. Some are loved, some are unloved and have become ruins themselves. But Rowen's theatre endures, and it will for centuries to come. I can't wait to go back and see a performance there myself.

I'll just be sure to dress warmly!

# CHAPTER NINE
## CADGWITH

Until we visited this lovely Cornish seaside village on our drive, I had never heard of it. Our hosts, who were showing us around Cornwall, were quick to inform us that this village was quite famous to most Britons. It is known as a 'typical' seaside Cornish village, and scenes of its boats in the harbor adorn calendars all over Britain. Like Gold Hill in Shaftesbury, Dorset, it's an iconic scene. Like a moth to a flame, I knew I would have to visit because I rather like iconic scenes, especially ones that might not be known to Anglotopia's readers.

Cadgwith is almost a secret place. Normal traffic isn't allowed, you have to use a car park and then walk down a footpath to get into the village. Along the way you'll spot beautiful thatched cottages battered by the sea over the centuries. The village is compact, and you can see it all in an afternoon. There isn't much to actually do other than wander around and admire the beauty of the place. We peeked into an old Cornish tin church, which had a quiet beauty about it. And that's what I would ascribe to the entire place – it has a quiet beauty to it, only interrupted by the sound of the sea lapping on the cliffs beyond.

Cadgwith is 'old Cornwall' and is one of the last places to see the traditional way of life still operating in plain view. The village has its origins in medieval times as a collection of fish cellars in its sheltered southeast facing the coastal valley, with a small shingle beach and cove. Fishing subsidized local farmers' livelihoods. Cadgwith was originally called 'Porthcaswydh,' becoming 'Por Cadjwydh' in Late Cornish, and is derived from the Cornish word for a thicket, literally meaning battle of trees, probably because the valley was densely wooded before it was cleared for settlement. From the 16th century, the village became inhabited, with fishing as the main occupation. Subsequently, houses, lofts, capstan houses, and cellars constructed of local stone or cob walls and thatched or slated roofs were built along the beach and up the sides of the valley leading to Cadgwith's characteristic Cornish fishing village appearance. In recent times a very small Anglican church was built, next to the path from the car park down to the seafront, dedicated to St Mary.

Cadgwith exists because of fishing. Until the 1950s, the town was known for fishing pilchards, a kind of sardine that was a staple of Cornish diets. When you observe the cliffs around the village you can spot a small hut at the very top. There were two of these huts, each manned during the day. They were called 'huers' - from the Cornish 'Hevva, Hevva! which translate as 'here they are!' It was their job to keep watch over the sea during pilchard season, and when the shoals of pilchards were spotted, they would sound the alarm. The entire village would then mobilize and head out to sea to harvest the riches before them. They would use a special netting technique using large seine boats and seine nets, which was a system used to enclose the large shoals of pilchards. In 1904 a record 1,798,000 pilchards were landed over four days.

That was the high point for pilchard fishing. They were overfished, and a changing climate moved the pilchard shoals. Fishing them was no longer economically viable, so the town's fleet switched to brown edible crabs, spider crabs, lobsters, sharks, monkfish, and conger eel.

Fishing in Cadgwith is rather unique in that there isn't much of a protected harbor for the boats to anchor or secure to a quayside. Instead, the boats pull right up onto the beach at the end of the day. To do this, they use a massive old Victorian engine that pulls each boat up with a giant metal chain. The men who fish out of Cadgwith have done so for generations, with many boats passed down from father to son. In the competitive world of industrialized shipping, the fishermen of Cadgwith are an anachronism that are increasingly under threat. If fishing can't pay the bills, people will not do it.

The village itself has already pivoted. There are more holiday lets in Cadgwith than there are fishermen. Its pretty thatched cottages and easy access to the sea, with plenty of places to walk, make Cadgwith very popular with tourists. This, like a lot of towns and villages, can make the place seem rather empty. But the fisherman of Cadgwith endure. They were recently included in a documentary TV series that featured their ancient way of life and showed their salty ways enduring in our modern world.

They even turned to the 21$^{st}$ century invention of crowdfunding to help preserve the Cadgwith fishing fleet.

See, the fisherman did not own the huts, equipment, and sheds on the beach they relied on to continue to fish. They were at risk of being sold off and turned into more holiday lets. So the fisherman banded together with the village and launched a crowdfunding campaign. The goal was to raise the money needed to buy one of the buildings so that at least part of the fishing fleet could continue. Because what would Cadgwith be without the picturesque fishing boats pulled up on the shingle beach?

Thanks to the attention of the documentary series and the national media, the money came flooding in (and I will admit that Anglotopia also donated funds to the cause as this happened a few years after our visit, and the place is quite special to me now). Not only did they raise the money to buy the building, they raised further funds to buy all the fishermen's huts on the beach and equipment, with enough money to renovate them and preserve them for future generations of fishermen. There's hope in these old villages yet.

Maritime history is strong here, and you can even see it in the cottages. Old stone cottages feature stained glass images of the sea and old sailing ships. There's a local pub, gift shops, ice cream shops, and cafés. I'm sure in the summer it's bustling. When we visited, it was as quiet as a morgue. It was pleasant. Just the sound of your voice and the sea on the rocks in the cove. You can freely walk amongst the chains and boats sitting on the beach; it's an open workplace, though do take care where you step, and if they're operating the beach winch, I would stay clear - it could take off a limb! If you're lucky, you'll come across a salty old fisherman repairing nets, as we did. He was perfectly friendly, at least I think he was, as his thick Cornish accent is a challenge to understand.

*Jonathan Thomas*

# CHAPTER TEN
## The RNLI

Like many places we visited in Cornwall, we parked at the top of town then walked down into St Ives. It was a lovely walk through a labyrinth of narrow alleys and streets leading down to the bustling harbor area. We had to rely on the local knowledge of our guides because we would have had no idea how to navigate the narrow lanes. If we'd lost them, I imagine we'd still be wandering the alleys of St Ives looking for them, five years later. When we got to the bottom, we were presented with a bustling seaside town filled with tourists, shops, restaurants, and beautiful, picturesque cottages.

It was achingly beautiful. It was exactly what I expected from a Cornish seaside town.

St Ives has a long and fascinating history that dates back to the prehistoric era, as most places in Britain do. Evidence of human settlements has been found in the area, including a Neolithic burial chamber and Iron Age fortifications. The town's location on the coast made it an important center for fishing and trade, and it played a significant role in the tin and copper mining industries that were once prevalent in Cornwall.

During the Middle Ages, St Ives grew in importance as a trading port, with merchants from all over Europe visiting to buy and sell goods. The town also played a role in the defense of the coast, with its strategic location making it an important site for fortifications.

In the 19th century, St Ives became a popular destination for artists, who were drawn to the town's natural beauty and picturesque surroundings. Its narrow streets, quaint cottages, and stunning coastline provided endless inspiration for artists and many well-known painters, including J.M.W. Turner and Walter Sickert, spent time in St Ives.

The 20th century brought significant changes to St Ives, with the decline of the mining industry and the rise of tourism. The town's reputation as an artistic hub continued to grow with the establishment of the St Ives School of Painting in 1938. The school attracted a new generation of artists, including Barbara Hepworth and Ben Nicholson, who helped to establish St Ives as a center for modern art. It even now hosts its own outpost of the Tate!

Today, St Ives remains a popular tourist destination, known for its stunning beaches, picturesque harbor, and vibrant arts scene. We were delighted to be there for the first time. We had a lovely lunch on the beach, in the glorious sunshine, followed by a stroll through the town – where we did a spot of shopping in the unique local shops (and picked up a few souvenirs that we still cherish). The place was bustling, even for a weekday on the tail end of the tourist season. It was the perfect time to be there. Not too hot, not too cold, with a light salty breeze off the harbor.

The sea is at St Ives, and St Ives is the sea. When you go down to the main harbor, you're presented with the massive stone building housing the town's RNLI lifeboat (Royal National Lifeboat Institute). The rather large boat is perched in its housing, with the doors open, waiting to be called into action at a moment's notice.

The RNLI feels ever present in Cornwall. Perhaps it's because Cornwall is surrounded by water on three sides, and it sits at the confluence of the English Channel, the Atlantic Ocean, and the Irish Sea. They're notoriously rough waters that have been a graveyard for ships for centuries. The organization has played an important role in Cornwall's life and history. Everyone knows a volunteer for the RNLI. Everyone knows of someone who's been rescued while in distress.

All around Cornwall, and really all around of coast of Great Britain and Ireland, you will find a series of lifeboat sheds right on the water, ready to launch rescue boats at a moment's notice. Staffed completely by volunteers, the RNLI are the sentries of the seas around Britain, ready to save any life, no matter where they come from. It is one of Britain's most beloved institutions. When we explored Cornwall, we saw the RNLI everywhere - and the evidence of it - from abandoned lifeboat sheds to active ones like the one in St. Ives, home to a massive rescue ship, to the tiny one in Port Isaac.

The Royal National Lifeboat Institution was founded in 1824 to provide a coordinated system of stations around the coastline of the British Isles to rescue sailors from ships in peril. With 237 stations manned by volunteers, the Institution relies on endowments and donations through collection boxes for its activities; they receive no public funding despite being

Britain's equivalent to the US Coast Guard. Over 140,000 lives have been saved since the Institution was founded by Sir William Hillary, who lived on the Isle of Man. The Institution had Queen Elizabeth II as its patron until her death (as of this writing, Charles III has not taken up the mantle of patron). The RNLI has been instrumental in the development of lifeboats and safety vests to protect both professional and amateur sailors from the hazards of the sea.

Since men first took to sea in boats, shipwrecks have been a regular and tragic hazard. Major shipwrecks, with large losses of life, became more common in the 19th century when shipping was the main method for transporting goods and people over significant distances. One notoriously dangerous place off the coast of England is the Isle of Man. This island lies between the east coast of England and Ireland, in the Irish Sea, and is surrounded by hidden reefs that are a potential graveyard for ships.

In the early years of the 19th century, the Isle of Man was home to Sir William Hillary, a minor noble who had managed to squander the large fortune he had inherited. Consequently, he was on the island to avoid his creditors, as well as the family of his irate first wife. Born a Quaker, but now not a practicing one, it may nevertheless have been his Quaker sensibilities that affected him when, on the night of the 14th of December, 1822, the Royal Navy ship HMS Racehorse foundered on rocky reefs off the south-east coast of the island. Five intrepid local men from Castletown, then the capital, made four trips to the wreck to rescue sailors, but in the end, six men from the ship and three of the rescuers drowned.

Accounts vary as to whether Sir William actually took part in the rescue or just heard accounts of it, but he was moved by the experience and decided to establish an organization that would provide rescue services not only on the Isle of Man but across Britain. In February of the following year, he published a pamphlet entitled An Appeal to The British Navy on the Humanity and Policy of Forming a National Institution for the Preservation of Lives and Property from Shipwreck. Pamphleteering was a common way of drawing attention to an issue at the time – printing a booklet that could be distributed widely to develop an interest in a cause. In making his appeal, he presented persuasive arguments based on using the latest tools available to rescue sailors.

For distressed ships to signal for help, he suggested the use of rockets, recently developed by the inventor and military rocket pioneer Sir William Congreve. To pull ships away from being blown onto reefs, he proposed the two-string kite system for which Charles Dansey had won a medal from the Royal School of Artillery just the year before. Kites were also used to carry lines to shore, but William Hillary favored for that the much more practical and successful Manby Mortar, a small cannon that fired a line from the shore, invented by George William Manby in 1808. Hillary also wanted to take advantage of the flag code recently developed for merchant shipping by the sailor and novelist Captain Frederick Marryat. Marryat's Code (precursor of the International Code of Signals) was the standard system used throughout most of the 19th century.

Despite this list of innovations, Hillary's appeal fell on deaf ears at the Admiralty. Undeterred, he decided to seek private support. A meeting was held on the 4th of March 1824, at The Tavern, on Bishopsgate Street in London. Besides Sir William, Thomas Wilson, MP for the City of London, and George Hibbert, ship owner and chairman of the West Indies Dock Company, were there. The West Indies Dock (today the site of Canary Wharf) was London's major merchant-shipping port, so Hibbert's interest in marine safety had a practical aspect. Today Hibbert's image is tarnished by his support for slavery.

The three men agreed to form the National Institution for the Preservation of Life from Shipwreck. King George IV agreed to be a patron, and the society received a Royal Charter in 1860. In 1854 the name had been changed to the Royal National Lifeboat Institution. There were already existing lifeboats around the coast of the British Isles by that time, typically manned by volunteers drawn from local sailors. There were believed to be 39 such boats in 1824 but, within one year, the RNLI had added 13 more. It actively encouraged and assisted in the establishment of more stations until, by 1909, there were 280 RNLI boats and only 17 independent boats around the coast.

Of course, to rescue sailors, lifeboats are needed, able to operate in rough seas, and the first ship specially designed for this was an 'unimmergible' boat, designed and patented by Lionel Lukin in 1785. He modeled his ship on some earlier French designs, and it had airtight compartments that kept it afloat even when completely full of water. Even though he was directly encouraged by King George IV, he too, like Hillary later, found his approaches to the Admiralty received no response. His work floundered when he entrusted his boat to a captain in Ramsgate for testing, but the captain found it much more useful for smuggling than for rescuing sailors. The first functioning lifeboat using his design was built in 1786 and used at Bamburg Castle, Sharpe, Northumberland. In 1851 Algernon Percy, 4th Duke of Northumberland, offered a prize of 100 guineas and attracted 280 entries for a lifeboat competition. The winning design was by James Beeching of Yarmouth for his 'self-righting' boat.

The Conister Shoals and St Mary's Isle lie off the harbor of Douglas on the Isle of Man. This was another 'hot spot' for shipwrecks and, although Hillary may not have been there for the wreck of HMS Racehorse, when he saw the packet-steamer St George being washed onto the Shoals on the stormy night of the 19th of November, 1830, he raced to the docks, put together a volunteer crew and set out in a lifeboat to rescue the ship. The lifeboat was almost swamped, and the 60-year-old Sir William was washed overboard, but eventually, after a great effort, the crew of 22 and all the 18 on the lifeboat made it safely back into Douglas Harbour. In all, Sir William is credited with being personally involved in saving 300 lives at sea.

In its early years, the Institution depended on private philanthropy, and when appeals by Sir William for government support were rejected as being 'a departure from the principle of private benevolence,' the Institution went through a period of some decline. It was only when the Duke of Northumberland stepped in as President at the same time as he became First Lord of the Admiralty that funding from the Privy Council for Trade was secured. Although this annual support of £2,000 only lasted for 15 years, it was during that time that the Institution was able to establish itself on a firm footing based on endowments and donations. It has continued to support itself in that way, and the familiar collection boxes in shops can be seen across the country, especially in coastal areas.

During WWI, volunteer boats of the RNLI carried out numerous rescues, although the single largest rescue was before that in 1907 when multiple crews from stations in Cornwall spent 16 hours rescuing 456 passengers from the ocean liner SS Suevic. During WWII, lifeboats of the RNLI took part in the evacuation of soldiers from Dunkirk in 1940, as well as rescuing many downed pilots during the Battle of Britain.

The RNLI has a system of Gold, Silver, and Bronze medals awarded to its members for bravery in rescues. The youngest recipient was Frederick Carter, who was 11 years old at the time. Grace Darling was the daughter of a lighthouse keeper who rowed the boat she and her father used to rescue nine people from the SS Forfarshire in 1838. She was praised for her heroism and awarded an RNLI Silver Medal for gallantry.

The RNLI isn't without controversy in this modern age when everything creates controversy on social media websites, no matter how good it is. When Britain experienced an uptick in migrants crossing the English Channel from France, it was criticized for saying it would rescue any boats that experienced distress. Despite the fact that this is the right thing to do and their primary mission, there were voices in Britain who took issue with this. The RNLI rightfully didn't back down and, in fact, experienced a surge of donations as people wished to show their support for this bastion of British humanity.

Today, Britain's coastal communities serve in the RNLI with pride and distinction, ready to go at the drop of the hat if they're called to sea to save a life. More than a few have died themselves in the service of saving those in distress in the sea. Many more people have been saved. Along with the National Trust, the RNLI is one of Britain's pillar cultural institutions, and that's why you will find donation jars as far inland as England's Midlands. If you see one, drop a few pounds in. The money always goes to a good cause.

*Jonathan Thomas*

# CHAPTER ELEVEN
## Doc Martin

Around 1999, a year that I guess now qualifies as ancient history, a location scout for an independent British film was looking for a quaint English village in which to shoot a movie. It needed to be small, it needed to be coastal. It needed to be relatively easy to get to and, most importantly, it needed a cooperative town to allow the disruption of a major film production. It helped if it was far enough off the beaten path so as not to attract too much attention during filming.

For all of these reasons, that scout decided on the small Cornish village of Port Isaac, a place that no one outside of Cornwall had probably ever heard of. The film in question was Saving Grace, and it starred Brenda Blethyn and Craig Ferguson (long before he moved to the USA and got famous here). A widow, hard on her luck, takes to growing marijuana to make ends meet. The film also starred another famous actor

- Martin Clunes - who was at the height of his popularity from the British TV comedy British Men Behaving Badly. The film was to be his introduction to the cinema.

It wasn't much of an introduction; it was a sleepy indie movie that didn't really go far (the film is just all right, frankly, in my opinion). Now, it's a footnote in British film and TV as a piece of trivia for the hit British TV show that came shortly thereafter - Doc Martin. You see, Clunes played a doctor in the film. And it led to several telefilms for Sky Television playing the same character, all filmed in Port Isaac. But after two films were shot, the studio financing them folded, and Clunes took the concept to a new network. Creative changes and a new direction led to the creation of Doc Martin, a new TV show concept, and a completely new character set in the same town now called Port Wenn. The show focuses on a fish out of water London doctor, moving to Port Isaac to get away from surgery and his fear of blood.

The show was an instant hit in Britain. In its third season, nearly 10 million people would tune in to each episode of the show. When it was imported to the USA by PBS as part of their Masterpiece schedule, it also became a huge hit. It became a background show that PBS would air over and over to fill airtime. So it built a strong following of American Anglophiles who loved the stories from quirky Port Wenn.

As with all shows like this, Americans wanted to visit the place where the show was filmed. Most would discover that Port Wenn doesn't actually exist. It's actually the village of Port Isaac, a sleepy fishing village on the north Cornish coast. Just about as far from London as you can get without being in Ireland. The show is filmed on a two-year schedule. It's filmed when the tourist season ends, and then it's usually aired the following year. When the Doc Martin train comes to town, the entire town becomes a film set. Lucky fans who accidentally timed their trips right have actually been able to watch the show being filmed. Then when filming is done, the crew disappears, and Port Isaac becomes a sleepy village again.

Well, not really, and I'll get to that.

Port Isaac likely has Celtic origins, like most of the rest of Cornwall. It doesn't have a founding date. It's one of those places in Britain where people have always lived because it was a good spot. The fishing from Port Isaac has always been good, and its sheltered harbor has been home to fishermen for centuries. The biggest industry was the pilchard industry, and at one point, there were 60 boats plying their trade from the harbor.

It was home to hard-working people who risked their lives on the rough seas around Cornwall - which took many lives every year. There's a reason there are so many lifeboat stations around these parts. Even to this day, the seas around Cornwall are treacherous. When the harbor wall was built during the reign of Henry VIII, Port Isaac became an important port where goods could be brought to shore and distributed throughout Cornwall. The village gained great wealth from shipping and fishing.

Most of the quaint cottages you see in the village today were built in the 18th and 19th centuries. Many are now 'listed' buildings, meaning they are protected. This keeps the village in a kind of historical aspic like a lot of places in Britain. It also creates problems for the locals as they can't construct new buildings within the old village, so Port Isaac has expanded in the cliffs above the village. By the early 20th century, once Port Isaac was connected to the rest of Britain by rail, its importance as a center of shipping and fishing began to fade away, and the village began an economic decline that has been replaced by the tourist trade. British tourists knew about the place long before American retirees did.

I didn't discover Doc Martin until the early Aughts. It was streaming on the Netflix service, and Jackie and I decided to try an episode to see if we liked it. The show came highly recommended by my parents (my father is not an Anglophile, but he loved the show). We were hooked after one episode and immediately binged all the available episodes, and we've been watching it since. The show has had its ups and downs, some seasons are better than others, and some of the plots have verged on the ridiculous. But all through the show, Port Isaac was the real star. Even with all the zany characters who lived there, Port Wenn was a sort of English utopia that many American Anglophiles wished they could live in.

So, when we were planning our drive, we knew that we would have to visit this special place, even though it wasn't really on the way or on the traditional LeJog route.

In my 20 years of travel to Britain, I'd never been there simply because of its remoteness. It's FAR away from London. And as I wrote about our epic five-hour drive to Cornwall, it takes a long time to get there. This is one thing that always surprises Americans seeking to visit Port Isaac; it's not easy to get to if you're not comfortable driving in the UK. Trains don't run there anymore. You can take a tour bus, but even that will require an all-day journey. You can't just dash down for the day from London. You have to commit to a few days in Cornwall, which is what we planned to do for this part of our drive.

Port Isaac would be our one major stop on the road from Cornwall to Castle Combe. It took us about 90 minutes to get there from where we were staying. That's one thing that struck me about Cornwall – it is a very, very big place. So much to see and explore (and yes, I know, three days was not enough, we will be back to Cornwall one day). So, we sat back and enjoyed the drive through the beautiful rolling countryside, with occasional peaks at the sea along the way.

Visiting in September, we didn't expect big crowds. We were absolutely wrong. The village was so crowded that there was nowhere to park. Our driver had to drop us in the center of the village and then park the car as close as he could (and everywhere in Port Isaac is uphill when you're done with the day). It was definitely a surprise to see how crowded the place was on a weekday in the off-season. I applaud all my fellow tourists who made the journey that far from London – it takes quite a bit to get there! The village was absolutely heaving but also buzzing.

We were lucky that it was a beautiful sunny day. However, it was cold, and the wind off the Atlantic Ocean was quite fierce, but you really only felt it in the more exposed areas. We were so cold, in fact, that Jackie had to buy a jacket. We didn't expect Britain to be this chilly in September, and it wasn't forecasted to be so chilly, but the storm that came in brought cool weather with it. Because of this, we didn't bring warm jackets, just a few sweaters. But with the expected cold, we figured that by the time we got up to Scotland, it'd be much colder. Being the sensible woman she is, Jackie bought a waxed jacket from the gift shop located within the old schoolhouse building where they shoot exteriors for Doc Martin. That coat would end up keeping her warm for the rest of the trip (and to this day it is very durable).

Port Isaac really is very much nestled into its little cove and the village has capitalized on the Doc Martin craze. Many of the shops are geared toward visitors who are fans of the show (see aforementioned jacket purchase). There are guided walking tours. We didn't have time to do something like that, but the village is not large, so you can easily wander around and see all your favorite shooting locations.

It was heaving with tourists that day, but we managed to get around easily enough, and we only had a short wait when we decided to stop for lunch. We ate at Port Isaac Pottery & Chapel Café. It was a strange little place – it was clearly a former church, but it was also a shop selling lamps and food. The food was very, very good. I had my first Cornish pasty, and I'm in love now. We walked up the hill and, of course, visited the cottage where the Doc's office is located. Fern Cottage is probably one of the most famous cottages in Britain now. It's actually a holiday let; you can rent the cottage and sleep in it. But don't rent it thinking that it looks anything like the doctor's surgery on the inside. It doesn't. The interiors are filmed on a set in a barn outside Port Isaac.

One thing I knew I had to try while we were in Cornwall was a Cornish pasty. You can find them pretty readily anywhere in Britain, but I'd never tried one, and the only true Cornish pasty is one you can get in Cornwall. The pastry is an interesting dish. It's workmen's food. Cornwall has long been known for its mineral wealth (see the show Poldark). Tin mining was the first major industry, and there is evidence that there was tin mining even in the era of Roman Britain. Tin mining was dangerous work but also toxic. The miners would find themselves covered in shards of tin. This made eating difficult as they knew you didn't want to ingest the raw metal (being exposed to it was bad enough).

So they devised a very British solution to the problem. They put the food into a half-moon-shaped meat pie with hearty meats, veg, and gravy. Then they crimped the rounded edge into a hard crust. Miners could then hold the pasty by the crust, eat their entire pie and not have to touch the actual food they were eating. It was a sensible and innovative dish that was also delicious. It became popular in Britain far and wide. Now the crust is no longer there for you to really hold, it just adds to the flavor.

The Chapel Café had them on the menu, so I ordered one. It arrived on a cutting board, hot out of the oven with fresh salad and chunky chips. I cut into it, it was a steak pasty, and put it into my mouth; at first I didn't taste anything because it was so hot that I momentarily lost the ability. When my sense of taste returned, it was delicious. Hot, filling, and with chunky chips, it was the perfect Cornish lunch. I'm now a convert. I want pasties all the time now! I've even ordered them from specialist makers here in the USA (though they're just not the same as having one in Cornwall!).

After we'd eaten and after we'd seen the Doc's house, we realized that we'd pretty much seen all Port Isaac had to offer, and we really needed to hit the road to get to Castle Combe (well, actually Bristol, to get our hire car so that we could begin our driving part of the trip). So we began the long trek uphill from the harbor to the car park above the town. The crowds lessened and lessened the higher we went. The village became quiet, and we began to see what it was like to actually live there.

And the conclusion was not good. We didn't encounter any locals at all on our way back to the car park. Most of the houses appeared empty - many had signage indicating they were self-catering holiday lets or Airbnb properties. I imagine it would be quite nice to stay here and enjoy the rhythms of the village. But I suspect there isn't much of village life left if all the cottages are holiday homes and holiday lets. This is a problem throughout Cornwall (and really any beautiful place in Britain). The locals can no longer afford to live there. So they become empty, sanitized places geared to tourists. It's a shame. And I felt guilty being one of them that day.

    We all watch Doc Martin to escape to Port Wenn, and it's a bucolic English Utopia, but it doesn't really exist. The show is a fantasy. Still, I quite liked visiting it in person for the day. I should note that after our trip, they filmed two further seasons of Doc Martin, and then the show finally ended after ten seasons and 79 episodes. The show will live on in endless PBS repeats. It's possible that tourism and the damage it causes to places like Port Isaac will abate a little bit, but I'm sure the tourism economy generated by it will continue for many years to come. It may become a little quieter. A little sleepier. A little more like the fictional show set there. That certainly won't be a bad thing.

*Jonathan Thomas*

# CHAPTER TWELVE
## TO BRISTOL

Does driving through a place and not stopping count as visiting a place? We had to get from Cornwall to Bristol, a very long drive. In fact, it's half the time it takes to get from Cornwall to London. The plan was to pick up our rental car in Bristol, the perfect halfway point for us to begin our drive properly on our own, as we would have the whole rest of the drive ahead of us. Our friends needed to get home and could no longer chauffeur us around endlessly (though we didn't want it to end!). We were, and still are, so incredibly grateful for the locals' eye view of Cornwall. But I was itching to get behind the wheel myself.

After we left Port Isaac, we hopped onto the main A road and headed for Bristol. The plan originally had been to stop at Tintagel Castle, the legendary birthplace of King Arthur, on the way. But after expending a considerable amount of energy wandering around hilly Port Isaac, and being quite full from a Cornish pastry lunch, we decided to save it for a future trip and head on. The day was getting away from us.

We drove the length of Cornwall but frankly didn't see much of it other than what you can from the car window along the main road. We did not make any stops. We didn't have time. Unfortunately, Devon got the same treatment. It was not on the itinerary for this trip, and neither was Somerset. It pained me greatly to just skip by these beautiful and vibrant counties, but we simply didn't have time to explore them. Still, it was a joy to watch them pass by along the motorways.

So, no, I don't consider us having actually visited these places, which is a good enough reason to go back when we can.

It's strange, really. England is not a huge country. But driving any great distance makes it feel like it is enormous. Perhaps traffic moves slower than in the US. But perhaps it's the changes in the landscapes that make Britain feel like such a wide-open place. Back home in Indiana, I can drive for four hours in any direction and pretty much see the same thing: endless corn or soybean fields with an occasional town. In the three hours it took to get from Port Isaac to Bristol, we passed from the rocky shoreline to dense moors through Bodmin, green hills, flat pastures through Somerset, rivers, and floodplains. It was truly glorious. There was no looking at my phone on this journey; there was far too much to see out the car window.

I was rather grateful I wasn't doing the driving on this section of the trip because it afforded me the opportunity to see the one thing I love the most about Britain, the landscape. Years later, whenever I was stressed about things (especially during the dark days of COVID-19 in Spring 2020), I simply needed to stop, close my eyes, and remember this drive. In terrible moments, with just a thought and a few moments of mindfulness, I would be back in the back of that Volvo with our friends, with ClassicFM playing on the radio and the green English countryside rolling on by. Endless beauty. Endless contentment.

Once we got to Bristol, the fun began. It's usually easiest to pick up a rental car at an airport, as that's where most are usually located. So, months before, once our itinerary with our friends was settled, I reserved an affordable automatic car with Hertz (the company we usually rent from when we travel). When we arrived at Bristol Airport, the place was a mess. It was under construction, and the signage was not accurate in any way.

It also became clear quite quickly that the rental car pick-up flow at the airport was designed for passengers coming off an airplane, not showing up in another car, and picking something up. Once we figured that out, I simply got out of the car and walked through the car park like I was an arriving passenger. I found the Hertz area of the car park. But that was not where you checked in to pick up your reservation. No, that was in a completely different building by the terminal.

So, more walking. I walked around the massive parking garage until I found the OTHER Hertz desk and checked in to get my car. At this point I was quite irritated and ready to just get the car keys and go, but was told that they were short on cars and that I was getting a free upgrade to what was available.

"Fine," I said with trepidation. The last time this happened to me I was given a sports car, instead of an economy compact car, and ended up with a false claim against me for damage to the wheels that was there when I rented the car (I won the dispute). I did not particularly want to repeat the situation. They handed me the key, I went through the doors, and there it was.

The most beautiful, fully-kitted-out Land Rover Discovery I'd ever seen. It was quite a departure from what I'd rented, but I was delighted that I would get to drive a Land Rover for our journey across Britain. What's more fitting than driving one of the most British cars there is, that's made in Britain, across the entire island? I talk more about Land Rover in a later chapter, so I won't go deeply into the car now.

When I returned to our friends, waiting in the other Hertz car park with Jackie, everyone was quite shocked to see this massive, brand-new vehicle pull up. I couldn't believe our luck. A massive luxury Land Rover for the price of an economy compact car! What luck!

BUT!

I have been here before so, before we bid farewell to our friends until dinner later, I hopped out of the car and took a detailed picture of every surface and had the Hertz attendant confirm that it was scratch and dent-free.

Finally, I got behind the wheel, mounted our cameras and recording equipment, and we were on our way. I was very excited to be behind the wheel and on our way to Castle Combe, our stop for the night.

We promptly hit Bristol's rush hour traffic and sat on the road in the pouring rain. A drive that normally takes 30 minutes took us almost an hour and a half.

I couldn't have been enjoying myself more!

When we eventually arrived in Castle Combe, it was still raining. In fact, rain would be a feature for most of the rest of the trip. We parked the car, grabbed our bags, and checked in for our evening stay at the Castle Inn Hotel, right in the center of Castle Combe. I was thrilled to finally be there with Jackie, as I'd stayed there once before without her and was terribly lovesick missing her. It's the most romantic little hotel with four poster beds, and with the soft rain outside, the absolute quiet of Castle Combe was heaven. I think of that moment often.

One of those perfect little moments that life gives you that you can go back to in your memory when times are really hard. It was heaven.

# CHAPTER THIRTEEN
## Castle Combe

There are places in England that epitomize what the country is to the outside world. Castle Combe, a small village in the Cotswolds, is one of those places. I have visited several times, and I knew when we were planning our trip that it would be the perfect place to stop as it was sort of halfway between Cornwall and Northern England. But really, I wanted any excuse to visit Castle Combe simply because it is so beautiful.

Nestled within the Cotswolds is one of the United Kingdom's greatest treasures. It is one of the romantic images of the English countryside that comes to everyone's mind (the English would describe it as 'chocolate box,' I think we would say it looks like something out of a Thomas Kincade painting). The quaint parish has old yellow stone buildings, lush foliage, and winding rivers. But what about Castle Combe captured the imagination and elevated it to a symbol? What keeps people coming to visit? What will they do when they get there?

If you visit on a day when there are few tourists, what you get is a quiet place, set apart from the world, enjoying a peaceful life. It was once the type of village that had everything you would need to live there - a shop, post office, pubs, schools, etc. It is not really that place anymore. The shops are gone now, there are still a couple of pubs. But not many people actually live here. Many houses have been turned over to holiday lets. Anyone can stay here for the price of an Airbnb.

If you visit on a day when there are plenty of tourists, you can barely move about the place because it will be heaving. Everyone flocks here to see how beautiful the place is. And that's entirely the attraction. It is pretty, so people want to see it. There's not really anything to actually do there, for the tourist anyway. But on several visits, I have learned that there actually is. You just need to visit when the tourists aren't there.

Castle Combe is a microcosm of British history. It's a place where people have always lived. Back before recorded history. Long before the village came into existence, Celts had settlements here. It is nestled in a wooded valley with plenty of water running through it, making it an attractive place for a settlement. Invasion of Britain by the Romans saw the construction of a fort due to its close proximity to Fosse Way (the main Roman road in these parts). After their desertion of England, the Saxons repurposed the fort. The Saxon victory at the Battle of Dryham led to a relatively peaceful period of 300 years. It was during this time that Saxons settled the valley, which they called "Cumbe," the Old English word for "valley." Over time, the spelling morphed into Combe.

With the Norman Invasion of 1066, King William I established the "Manor of Combe" for his loyal follower,

Humphrey de L'isle. The village was later recorded in the Domesday Book in 1086. Castle Combe Castle is believed to have been built sometime in the 12th century by Reginald de Dustanville after the manor passed to him. It was a motte-and-bailey castle believed to have five baileys rather than the normal four. The castle has long since fallen into ruin, and the earthworks and some of the stones remain. Castle Combe Castle was designated an ancient monument in 1981 for its historical importance and some minor artifacts that have been found there, such as arrowheads, buckles, spurs, and Saxon coins.

The surrounding village thus formed to service the castle. Today, in addition to several historic buildings, the village has a total of 47 homes. Its oldest structure is the Market Cross, erected sometime in the 14th century in the center of the village after it was granted the right to hold a market. The cross features a roughly one meter stone pedestal on two steps which is covered by a pyramid-like wooden roof supported by four stone columns. The villagers repaired it in 1590 and, at one point, it adjoined a Market House which was torn down in the 19th century as part of a road widening project. It is classified both as a historical monument and a Grade II listed structure.

The nearby St. Andrew's Church is a Grade I listed building that came into being about 100 years later. The church itself looks rather out of place and grand for a small village like Castle Combe. That's because The Cotswolds developed into a thriving wool-based economy which created wealth that is hard to imagine now. As a result, many 'wool cathedrals' were built - outsized churches for small villages simply because they were so wealthy. St. Andrew's is a rather lovely example and, if you time your visit right, you'll be the only one exploring it. It's also home to one of the oldest clocks in England which, though it has no face, controls when the bells toll.

Around the same time as the Norman castle fell into ruin, the Manor House was constructed. This great estate was the seat for the Barony of Combe and, over the centuries, had many owners, including famous historical figure Sir John Fastolf, on whom Sir John Falstaff in Shakespeare's Henry IV (Parts I and II), Henry V, and The Merry Wives of Window is based. Falstof was lord of the manor for 50 years and helped to promote its industry, including wool, which helped clothe King Henry V's armies in France. The barony ended around 1947, about the time that the Manor House was sold. It was later converted into a hotel that continues to operate.

Building upon its wool industry, Castle Combe became well-known for its textiles, and the red and white cloth of the village could be found in markets as far away as Cirencester, Bristol, and London. The Bybrook river had been a major resource in getting these goods out of the village but as it slowed in the 16th century the textile industry moved to other nearby communities. The prosperity of Castle Combe was responsible for the construction of many of the stone buildings that line its roads. Some of the village's most picturesque buildings date from later centuries, such as Dower House, which itself is a Grade II listed building.

In modern times, all of this history and natural beauty led to Castle Combe being named "The Prettiest Village in England" in 1961. It has been photographed a million times over, and has featured in art galleries and on calendars. It has also been a much sought-after place for filming productions such as Doctor Doolittle, War Horse, The Wolfman, and Stardust. It's a place that many Anglophiles will have seen before, whether in films or on TV or a calendar. It's idyllic England.

Our visit was punctuated by rain. It was raining when we arrived, and it was raining when we were leaving. This means that we practically had the place to ourselves. It was a special treat. We stayed at the Castle Inn Pub, where we usually stayed. It's a pub with rooms, but very nice rooms. It's owned by the nearby Manor House Hotel, so it acts as a sort of overflow hotel - and has rooms to match the reputation of the 'big house.' You'd think the place would be noisy because their rooms are above a pub. It is not.

I quite like the food at the pub, so it's very nice to be able to stay and eat at the same place. We invited friends to join us for dinner and had a grand time. We had the pub to ourselves and enjoyed a lovely meal.

My favorite thing about places like this is just how quiet they are.

Even as we clambered around the narrow and twisting corridors to get to our room, we were amazed at how quiet the hotel was during our stay. Our room was exactly what you'd want when you stay in the Cotswolds. It was spacious and featured an old English Oak four-poster bed. The bathroom was capacious with a very large bathtub, and there was a desk where I could work. We were right above the pub, with a view out onto the empty main street of Castle Combe, and the old Market Cross . The windows had original glazing, hundreds of years old, blurry yet clear in their imperfections. They creaked when you opened them. As we sat down to rest, the light rain outside made the most sublime noise as it hit the old stonework.

When we went to sleep that night, there was only silence in the village, with a little bit of rain on the old stone building to soothe us to sleep. We slept like the dead. In fact, I can confidently say I haven't had as good a night's sleep since. I decided long ago to embrace the hyperbole in my writing.

When I woke up the next morning, I wanted to wander around the village and take some pictures. I already had pictures of the place from previous visits, but why not take more? It was pouring down rain, so it was quite a contrast to my last visit when the sun was shining. One of my favorite pieces of video I shot on the entire trip was a short clip of the rain in Castle Combe. When I want to relax, I pull up the video and play it on repeat.

The Cotswolds are a very desirable area - featuring some of the most expensive property prices in Britain. Many of Britain's rich and famous, once they tire of London life, will buy a second home in The Cotswolds and pretend to live a 'country life.' A good example of this is Jeremy Clarkson, who now owns a 1,000-acre farm nearby (though, to be fair, he has thrown himself into farming fully and the Clarkson's Farm TV show is incredibly watchable). This desirability can make many pretty towns and villages in The Cotswolds feel rather deserted, which is a shame. It's easy to think the place is tucked away, hidden from the world - especially Castle Combe - but it absolutely is not. The Cotswolds are one of the most popular places to visit in Britain with both British and international tourists.

It is an idyllic, picture postcard England for both.

We've seen a lot of the Cotswolds over the years, from top to bottom and east and west. It's an area that we can happily return to again and again but, if you only have a day or two, a stopover in Castle Combe is very much worthwhile. If only to see what a real place The Cotswolds are and experience their perfection for just a moment.

And while today The Cotswolds are mostly a fantasyland, it will likely return to that idyllic England one day. After all, the place has been there for over 1,000 years. Trends come and come. Perceptions come and go. Communities come and go.

But its beautiful honey-colored buildings are not going anywhere.

I can't wait to return.

# CHAPTER FOURTEEN
## A Meditation on Motorway Services

One aspect of this trip that I was very excited about was that on our journey we would see many motorway services throughout Britain.

Yes, really.

Bear with me here.

As we drove on from Castle Combe on our way north, it was pouring down rain (you will notice a trend on this journey). We had a long drive ahead of us for the day – our plan was to reach York, but that was a four hour journey from the Cotswolds. So we planned to stop around halfway there at Hardwick Hall in Derbyshire. But on the way traffic was moving slowly and, before we knew it, we'd been in the car for a few hours. We needed the toilet and, thinking ahead to our arrival at Hardwick Hall, we were going to need umbrellas.

So, appearing on the horizon was a motorway services, and we were very excited to stop.

Britain's motorway services are a marvel of the motoring world, and this is coming from someone who lives in the land of massive truck stops. The primary reason is because motorway services are primarily for car drivers in Britain, whereas in America truck stops are geared toward long-distance truck drivers. Britain is a small enough country that people can drive to all points within it in a few hours. While Americans generally love to drive and have no problems doing so for 10 hours instead of taking a plane, most people still fly these days to far-flung destinations. They don't really use truck stops beyond refueling and using the toilet. Truck drivers do.

That's what makes motorway services special; they're for drivers. And they're lovely. Imagine an airport terminal, but at the side of the busy road - with all the conveniences you will need on a break from driving - hot food, groceries, fuel, toilets, clothing, and anything you may have forgotten to pack (for example, as I mentioned, we forgot umbrellas and, as we drove north through England in the driving rain, we realized we would need some). Some motorway services even have a motel on site. I've never seen a truck stop with a motel on site, though there are often ones nearby.

On Interstate 65 in Indiana, halfway between Chicago and Indianapolis, there's a rest stop in the middle of nowhere. By rest stop, I mean it's a shack where you can relieve yourself and has a selection of vending machines, half of which will be out of order at any given time. The bathrooms are not a place you wish to linger in or use if you don't have to. And most people, when getting to this point in the nowhere that is the Indiana countryside, will not bother to stop – instead, they will not relieve themselves until they need to refuel. The bar for rest stops for me is very low because of their quality in Indiana and throughout the USA. Truck stops are even worse places.

It doesn't have to be that way.

Britain can show us how it's done.

Throughout our journey we stopped at motorway services that were a treat. There was the brand new one right at the Cornish border, which served as a sort of border station entry point to Cornwall from the rest of England. It has plenty of places to get hot food, clean bathrooms, and various toys and sundries you may have forgotten to pack for your holiday. Even our English hosts were impressed by the new motorway services in Cornwall.

The concept of motorway services in Britain is relatively new - as are the motorways themselves. With the construction of Britain's first motorways in the 20$^{th}$ century, people from all over the UK found the country open in new ways. Post-war prosperity brought an increased number of drivers and necessitated a place where they could get gas, use the toilet, and maybe have a bite to eat. In the heyday of the motorway, these motorway service stations transformed from your average rest stop into tourist attractions in their own right.

Britain's motorway network kicked off with the opening of the M1 in 1958. Stretching from London to Leeds, the Ministry of Transport recognized that the new motorway would need some kind of services for travelers over their long journey. Owen Williams, the designer of the M1, visited the United States and took his design cues from the rest areas he found here along the Interstate. The ministry initially sent out a survey to 300 interested catering and motoring firms to help decide what sites might be the most suitable.

The questionnaire asked the firms which of the five sites they would prefer, the facilities they would provide, and what regulations they thought were appropriate. Sixty-seven of the 300 firms responded. Most of them pointed out the need for automobile repair and first-aid facilities, though some went so far as to recommend an ice cream stand or motels that would have taken up the whole area. The ministry chose to extend offers to Blue Boar (a forecourt/convenience store operator) and Forte (a hotel and restaurant company). The firms also wanted to put the initial stations at Redbourn and Watford Gap, but the ministry felt that would leave too large a gap between stations, so they went in a different direction.

The two locations the ministry approved were Watford Gap and Newport Pagnell, which were more evenly spaced out to serve motorists. Both stations opened some limited services on November 2, 1959, and Newport Pagnell became the motorway station to be able to fully service all traffic on August 15, 1960. Watford Gap was run by Blue Boar until it was sold in the 1990s, and Newport Pagnell by Forte. Located right at the point where Southern England bordered the Midlands, Watford Gap became a cultural icon that was synonymous with crossing over from the south to the north.

At first, the stations were just a place to grab a quick bite or cup of tea and use the bathroom (also known as a "tea and pee"). Both stations were designed with different crowds in mind. Watford Gap was intended for lorry drivers with quick service and the ability to get in and get out quickly. Newport Pagnell, on the other hand, was designed more for families with sit-down table service restaurants. The initial customers were more up-and-coming business types who had to travel a lot for work, but that quickly changed. Over time, Watford Gap began to share its name informally with the management company Blue Boar and became a stop so popular with 60s rock bands that Jimi Hendrix thought it was actually a concert venue.

The number of motorway services exploded into the early 60s, each trying to offer up new and interesting stations to travelers. One of the most well-known was Forton Services along the M6 near Lancaster, with its large air traffic control-like tower that housed the service station's main restaurant. I've actually been to this one as well (of course I have) and took several pictures of it (of course I did). It was strange pulling up to this flying saucer on the side of the motorway. Though I was disappointed to find out once inside that the tower was actually closed. Damn. When locals return home, they don't consider it home until they've seen the tower, standing silent sentry over the landscape.

The clientele became more varied as the years progressed and motorway services turned into microcosms of British society, with every group represented, from working-class families traveling in estate cars (we know them as "station wagons") to the "Gin and Jag" set out on an excursion in their luxury sports cars.

However, the good times were not to last. As the 60s wore on, the management companies behind the motorway services realized that the high-end amenities were proving less profitable. Food prices went up, quality went down, and a seedier group of customers started to take over. The lack of quality meals and the possibility of a run-in with football hooligans kept most motorists away well into the 1970s and 1980s. Towards the end of the 1980s, the motorway services attempted to mimic the popular chain restaurants that were springing up nearby but without much success.

Thus, in the 1990s, the motorway services decided to adopt the "if we can't beat them, join them" attitude, and many famous franchises, from Little Chef to McDonald's, began to take over the restaurant areas of the stations. Many also brought in well-known high street shops to lure customers, while others attempted to fill the gaps with local retailers and food service. Many of the companies that ran the services sold to larger conglomerates, such as Roadchef, Moto, Extra, and Welcome Break. However, these changes weren't enough for some customers who still felt that the motorway services represented a bygone era and remained cheap, dirty places. Opposition from local residents has led to very few new services being constructed since the 2000s.

However, public opinion has started to trend upward. One thing that has helped to change the quality of services is that Transport Focus has issued annual reviews of the motorway services since 2017. These reviews rank the services based on customer survey results and help travelers to find quality motorway services as well as educate the service providers about what customers want. Additionally, some of the older and more famous motorway services have achieved listed status, such as the Pennine Tower at Forton Services, which was granted Grade II listed status in 2012.

These are the motorway services I've come to love on my travels to Britain in the early 21st century. They're places where there is variety in food and shopping. No single one is the same as the others, which adds to the spirit of discovery. You can easily spend an hour or two at one of these places. They are places to slow down and enjoy your journey, have a cuppa and a piece of cake (or lunch). I'm convinced that electric cars will catch on better in Britain because when you have to stop to recharge, you won't mind hanging around for an hour in Britain's motorway services. I don't think you could say that about many truck stops in the United States of America.

One of the most innovative motorway services in the entire country is the Tebay Services on the border of

Cumbria. Started by a farmer who refused to sell his land for the motorway, it has become the best motorway services in the country. They have all the normal conveniences you expect - like clean toilets. But they also have a thriving business selling the food and produce of the Lake District. The Farmshop and Kitchen are so famous that truck drivers and motorists will go out of their way to stop there to pick up provisions or stop for a meal (their Sunday roasts are epic). The food store is run by a former Harrods grocer! Whom, I might add, has very high standards. The food sold in the place all comes from farms and producers throughout Cumbria, providing thousands of jobs. There are also very few food miles on the food as it doesn't travel far. Much of the beef and lamb served in the place comes from the very same farmer that founded the services.

It's hardly surprising that a five-part fly-on-the-wall documentary-style series on British TV about Tebay Services became one of the most watched shows of the year when it aired in 2021 (it's called A Lake District Farm Shop and if you can find it, it's worth watching.)!

The further north in Britain you get, though, the fewer motorway services you will come across. For one, the motorways don't extend much further than Edinburgh. The services become small petrol stations, pubs with rooms, or giant grocery store forecourts. They are obviously not nearly as exciting to stop at. But these are the places where you can get a real feel for the local character. A visitor from abroad is much rarer. But you'll also come across gems as we did in the middle of the Cairngorms National Park.

It was a strange wooden structure in the middle of the woods. We were desperate for the toilet and a cup of tea. It appeared almost out of nowhere. After driving for what felt like hours on the slow-moving A9 in Scotland (where average

*End to End*

speed cameras keep your speed low), we were ready to stop and stretch our legs. It was raining, but we didn't let that stop us from enjoying a bit of fresh Scottish air. The little place was bustling, and we got a fresh cup of tea, relieved ourselves, and visited the little onsite gift shop. It was a remarkable little mirage in the middle of the Scottish wilderness. It was not a motorway services, but it was still exactly what we've come to expect of any kind of services on our journeys in Britain.

Today, the motorway services all over Britain are bustling with life once again, returning to the clean and fascinating status that they once enjoyed. While the novelty has long since worn off, and they will never quite be at the level of fanciness they enjoyed in the early 60s, the services are still going strong, and there are locations all over Britain trying something different to stay relevant. Whether you need a toilet break, a bite to eat, or a chance to do a bit of shopping, the motorway services are there for travelers as they always have been.

*Jonathan Thomas*

# CHAPTER FIFTEEN
## Hardwick Hall

Hardwick Hall is unique among National Trust properties. Most are monuments to the men of British history (the good ones and the bad ones). Hardwick Hall is a monument to a woman and a very formidable woman at that. Elizabeth Shrewsbury, colloquially known as Bess of Hardwick, wielded power in an age when women did not have that much. Sure, England was ruled by a woman, but besides that, it was still uncommon for a woman to wield as much power as Bess of Hardwick. And her monument was Hardwick Hall. This remarkable Elizabethan structure, it is said, is more glass than brick.

When we were planning this trip I knew that, when we passed through the Midlands, I wanted us to stop off somewhere in the middle and have a break. Otherwise, the drive from the Cotswolds to Yorkshire would be too long. When I looked at the various maps I used to plan our trip I decided that it was finally time to visit Hardwick Hall; it is practically in the middle of our drive from Castle Combe to York. Perfect.

Well, almost perfect. It rained torrentially the entire day. But we would not let that ruin our enthusiasm to visit a stately home. After all, the British wouldn't let a little rain stop them from enjoying a grand day out in the English countryside.

After a couple of hours in the car, to be frank, we were quite ready for a break from driving. The problem was that on the back country roads to Hardwick Hall, we could not find a suitable spot to stop to freshen up. We hoped that on the way to the Hall, there would be a pub or anything that would be suitable. There was not. So, when we finally parked in the sodden field, acting as a car park for Hardwick Hall, we walked as quickly as we could to the Visitors' Center in the old stable block to get out of the rain and the mud.

It was still pouring while we ate lunch and, since it was raining, the café was packed from others avoiding the weather. Umbrellas we had picked up earlier at a motorway services proved very useful, and we stayed relatively dry. But, since it was raining, we decided to avail ourselves of lunch before continuing the trek over to the house, which we could not even see through the fog that had settled over the National Trust property. We had a wonderful National Trust café lunch and then a nice warm cup of tea, which was a welcome refreshment in the cold and damp. While we were eating lunch, the news was announced that there would be a Downton Abbey film entering production. In our line of work, this qualified as 'Breaking News,' a phrase we rarely get to use. I sat there with my iPhone, publishing the news to our website and Facebook page.

All in a day's work, eh?

After lunch, the rain had started to lighten up, and we began to walk to the hall itself, which was down a muddy gravel road and followed the walls that surrounded the property. When we entered the gate, I stopped in immediate awe. The sheer number of windows! It truly was impressive to look at. The rain started again, so we made our way inside. As the house is of great historical importance, the staff inside took our umbrellas and stored them for us so that we didn't go through the house with them.

The entrance deposits you in the main Tudor hall and it is quite a space. I'm always amazed by the high ceilings of these grand old houses. We wandered around and took pictures, as we normally do when we visit attractions like this. It was quite something to be in the home of Bess of Hardwick.

The 16$^{th}$ century in England was a turbulent and dangerous time. A time of religious conflict, intrigue, and plotting, where fortunes and lives could be won or lost on a whim and when anger, jealousy, and naked ambition directed state affairs as much as reason and strategy. It was also a time when women had opportunities previously denied them. With the first two female monarchs in the country's history, it was a century where it was acceptable for women to wield power and amass fortunes. Elizabeth Talbot, usually known as Bess of Hardwick, was pre-eminent in this age of new-found female power.

Bess was born around 1527 – the exact year is unknown, but recent research has uncovered court records that indicate 1527 – to John Hardwick of Derbyshire. At the time, this area between Lancashire and Yorkshire was heavily wooded and remote from the southern centers of power and influence. The family owned just a few hundred acres of farmland and were at the lower end of the social scale, being minor members of the gentry, just one step above yeoman farmers. Bess's younger brother James was the last male heir in the family.

Around 1543 Bess, perhaps very underage, was married to the 13-year-old Robert Barley, who was the heir to a nearby estate. However, he died at the end of 1544, and it seems the marriage was only on paper and that they never lived together or likely even consummated their marriage. Certainly, Bess was refused the dowry due to her when Robert died, and it was only after several years of court battles that she was awarded a share in the estate and compensation.

A few years later, in 1547, she married again, this time to a man twice her age who had himself been married twice before, his earlier wives having died. However, this was a more financially favorable marriage as her husband, Sir William Cavendish, was the King's Treasurer (to Henry VIII) and had amassed a significant fortune from Henry's seizure of church property known as the Dissolution of the Monasteries. Bess persuaded her new husband to sell his properties in the south and buy up the estates of her mother's second marriage in the Derbyshire district of Chatsworth. When Sir William died just 10 years later, Bess inherited his money since the land had been left to their six surviving children.

By this time, Henry VIII, Edward VI, and Mary I had come and gone, and Elizabeth I had taken the throne. Catholicism has been briefly and violently re-established by Mary, who imprisoned her half-sister, the future Queen Elizabeth, in the Tower of London. Spain had gone from Catholic enemy to husband of the Queen and back to the enemy again, and Britain had lost its last foothold in France, the port of Calais.

The Captain of the new queen's Guard and Chief Butler of England (basically the caterer to Royal Coronations) was Sir William St Loe and, when he married Bess in 1559, Lady

Cavendish became Lady St Loe. Unlike her earlier marriages, this seems to have been a loving one, and they were both around the same age. Sir William owned extensive estates in the south-west chiefly in Somerset and, although his death in 1565 without a male heir was likely the result of being poisoned by his brother, he left everything to Bess, turning her into one of the richest women in the country. Her annual income of £60,000 would be equivalent to around $10 million today. Not just wealthy, Bess also had power and influence with the new queen since she was one of Elizabeth's personal Ladies and had daily access to her. Because of her influence, wealth, and enduring good looks, she soon began to attract new suitors.

Bess took her time finding a suitable match but eventually, in 1568, now approaching 50, she and two of her children married into the powerful Talbot family in a triple ceremony. Bess married George Talbot, the 6$^{th}$ Earl of Shrewsbury, one of the most powerful men in the country. Her daughter, who was 12 at the time, married Talbot's oldest son and thus his heir, while her own son, 18, married one of Talbot's daughters, who was just eight years old. This would certainly have ensured that the Earl's fortune would pass into Bess's family.

Bess now became caught up in the intrigues of the British royals. Mary I of Scotland (not to be confused with Mary I of England) was considered by many British Catholics to be the legitimate heir to the throne. So, when she was deposed by rebellious Scottish lords and fled to England seeking Elizabeth's protection, the queen had a problem. She solved it by placing Mary in the hands of the Shrewsburys in what was effectively a house arrest. Mary spent the next 15 years living in several of the Shrewsbury estates, out of Elizabeth's way. She was ultimately executed for treason, but the years with Bess and her husband created marital strain and resulted in their separation. However, Bess and Mary also spent a considerable amount of time together working on embroidery and tapestry, as was appropriate to their gender and positions. Bess and the Earl had separated permanently by the time Elizabeth took Mary off their hands. The Earl died in 1590, leaving Bess the richest woman in England after Elizabeth herself and with the title Dowager Countess of Shrewsbury. She built herself a grand palace at Hardwick Hall to rival Elizabeth. The house is notable for its use of very large windows for the period.

While married to the Earl of Shrewsbury, Bess made complex marriage arrangements for one of her daughters, which resulted in a grandchild, Arbella Stuart, who was a potential heir to the throne. Bess's plan did not succeed and in the end she was forced to ask Elizabeth to take this willful child into her care after Arbella attempted to elope.

Bess died in 1608, outliving Elizabeth I and seeing James I take the throne and imprison Arbella Stuart in the Tower, where she eventually died after a plot by Sir Walter Raleigh to make her Queen – something Arbella had never personally wanted.

A woman of such power and wealth as Bess needed a grand house to make a statement. She needed a palace. She wanted to rival the power of her contemporary, Elizabeth I. She fancied herself a kind of 'Queen in the North' and set out to have a house that made such a statement.

After she married Sir William Cavendish, she convinced him to move back to her home county of Derbyshire; Bess was very fond of the scenery and the quiet environment. They purchased the property for their well-known home, Chatsworth House, in 1549 and began building in 1552. Chatsworth, as many of you probably know, is a jewel in the crown of Britain's stately homes. But it was not to last for Bess.

According to stories, Bess had a terrible argument with her husband, the Earl of Shrewsbury, and left their home at Chatsworth in 1584. She then organized plans to rebuild the Old Hall at Hardwick to create a new home for herself. However, her plans changed in 1590 when the Earl died, which left her with his inheritance. Due to her new positive financial situation, Bess decided to build a new construction at Hardwick, eliminating the renovation plans for the Old Hall altogether and creating the New Hall. She moved into her new house in October 1597. The Old Hall was left as a garden decoration and romantic ruin.

Her new Hardwick Hall was a true statement of her power and wealth. It contained numerous windows that were exceptionally large for the time period. Glass was a luxury - expensive to produce and heavily taxed, and the house was described as being more glass than walls. The chimneys were also built into the internal walls instead of being constructed on the outside. This was done to allow more room for the large windows without weakening the exterior structure. An added touch by Bess was the carved 'ES' initials that are present in six of the rooftop sculptures at the head of each tower. She wanted people to view her as a queen in her own right. There was no sign of other royalty in this house; it was Bess's house. And she wanted you to know it. All of this is still there, and it's quite something to see.

Hardwick is one of the first houses in England where the hall was built on an axis directly through the center of the house instead of at right angles to the entrance. The height of each ceiling is also unique, with each floor being slightly higher than the first. There are three main levels of the Hall, with the bottom level being smaller in height than the top floor. This was designed for the occupants of each room: the least important occupants stayed on the bottom floor, and the most important lived at the top. This helped to clearly designate the servants from the noble occupants.

The true treasure of Hardwick Hall is the remarkable contents inside that were collected by the Countess. An exceptionally unique collection of paintings and furniture from the 16th century are still present. The Hall is fully furnished, exactly as Bess would have kept it. The second floor of the house contains the largest Long Gallery that has ever been present in an English house. The most notable features are the tapestries and needlework on display. Much of the needlework art has the 'ES' initials, and it is therefore assumed that Bess herself created much of it.

Bess also created her own throne room - a place for her to hold court and use patronage to show her influence in the country.

After the death of Bess in 1608 her son William Cavendish, the 1st Earl of Devonshire, inherited Hardwick Hall. His great-grandson, also named William, was titled the 1st Duke of Devonshire, which began the dynasty. Chatsworth was and is the primary seat of the Dukes of Devonshire. However, Hardwick Hall remained a secondary home for the family to escape from the attention of the public. The family donated the house to the British government in 1956 in lieu of Death Duties, who then transferred the house to the National Trust, so it is now open for our enjoyment.

The Long Gallery was really something to behold. Even the pictures that I took don't do it justice. It's so vast. It's not just the length of the gallery - but the height of the ceilings as well. As it was a dreary and rainy day, we did not get the full effect of the hall or the other grand rooms. They were sparsely lit by unnatural light to protect the collection. So, we had a dark ghostly stroll through Bess's grand rooms. I can't decide if this was a disservice to the place or added to the dark Elizabethan atmosphere.

Despite the weather, it was surprisingly crowded inside. We encountered several of our countryfolk while we explored the various rooms open to the public. One American couple of retirement age basically shadowed our route through the house, and they were clearly in the midst of some kind of martial turmoil. They did not respect normal social distancing and were oblivious to everyone else while they worked through whatever marital tiff they were having. It was an embarrassment. Tut tut.

As with most of these places, we exited through the kitchens. We'd hoped to see the Old Hall as well, as I can never resist a good ruin. But alas, it was closed for restoration work. So I could only get a few ghostly pictures of it in the fog. Yes, Bess's house was most impressive. I would absolutely have to come back when the sun was shining to see her home in its full splendor, to see her full glory. And hopefully, avoid quarreling American couples.

# CHAPTER SIXTEEN
## YORK

The drive on to York from Derbyshire was long and wet. We drove through torrential rainstorms and spent a bit more time than we would have liked sitting in traffic as we'd managed to pass through the major conurbations of Northern England during rush hour. We did not see any of these cities. They were shrouded in clouds and rain. We only saw their traffic, which was a real shame.

Coming into York was a nightmare of traffic, but I was very excited to finally be there. In all my years of traveling to Britain, this was now the furthest north I'd ever been. It was all new territory for me. So, I got to soak it all in as we sat in single-file traffic in our giant vehicle, slowly snaking our way into York. We passed by the train station and then went through the hole they punched in the medieval city walls that surround the city so that cars could get through.

Our hotel was right there. The Grand Hotel and Spa was formerly the headquarters of the North Eastern Railway Company. Built in 1906, this building was a grand statement for Britain's richest railway at the time. Long redundant for Britain's current railway needs, the place was turned into a hotel in 2010, but not just any hotel a 'Grand' hotel. The former stately offices and meeting rooms have been turned into grand rooms and rather tony restaurants. It was quite a beacon to pull up to as the sun was setting, and we were exhausted after spending hours in traffic.

Upon entering our room, we were astounded by its unexpected grandeur. Although we had only booked a standard room, the ceiling towered at least 25 feet high, and the original windows added a touch of class. The room's design had a sleek and modern feel, with tasteful nods to train nostalgia and the history of the building. The lightning-fast Internet was a pleasant surprise, as it was comparable to our home's speed. We quickly uploaded all of our photos and videos, which would have taken almost a day's worth of time elsewhere. After finishing some work, we indulged in a delightful dinner at the onsite restaurant. The food was delicious, and the service was impeccable. As it was getting late, we retired to our room and alternated between work and luxuriating in the lavish bathtub. It it probably one of the most amazing hotels I've ever stayed in. A proper introduction to the ancient city of York.

Like several cities in the United Kingdom, the City of York can trace its origins back to the Roman Invasion, though Celtic tribes had settled the immediate area for centuries. Since the days of these early invaders establishing a settlement, York has grown to be one of the most important places in the country. It is the central authority for the county of Yorkshire, a cathedral city, and has had a major impact on the destiny of

Britain. The history of York is one worth exploring from its earliest settlers to the present day.

Mesolithic people settled the area around present-day York between 8,000 and 7,000 BC, but it's unknown whether these were temporary or permanent communities. Excavations in Yorkshire discovered stone axes dating back to the Neolithic period on the southwest bank of the River Oust, suggesting that people opted to live here well before the Romans came. Before the Roman legion arrived, the area had been settled by a tribe of Celtic Britons called the Brigantes. Their name meant "high ones," and they did not appear to keep any written records, with most accounts of the Brigantes tribes coming from the Romans as they advanced further north. The local Brigantes were amenable to their Roman neighbors at first but grew more hostile over time, necessitating the Ninth Legion to establish a permanent presence.

Romans first entered Yorkshire in 71 AD and settled the area between the River Ous and the River Foss. They brought 5,000 men comprising the Ninth Legion, who were led by General Quintus Petillius Cerialis, and built a fort there to provide defense and support against the Brigantes. The Romans gave it the name Eboracum which was the Latin form of the Britonnic name Eburākon, meaning "the place with the yew trees." During its time, the fort played host to Emperors Hadrian, Septimus Severus, and Constantinius I during their British campaigns and was the place where the latter two died, and their successions began. The community built up around the fort as support to the military forces with workshops, which didn't change as the Ninth Legion was replaced by the Sixth Legion. However, as with most of Britain, the Roman presence was not to last.

Beginning in 367 AD, barbarian attacks on the Romans

in the North started to drive the invaders back. By 400 AD, the garrison had abandoned the fort, and York's economy and population declined with it. With the withdrawal of the Romans from Britain, much history of this time period was lost, and there are no contemporary references to the city between 314 and 627 AD. It's believed that the locals dug new defensive ditches, and construction of the Anglian Tower began during this era. Welsh chronicles refer to the city and the kingdom it served as Ebrauc. Whatever York's fate, power abhors a vacuum, and the Anglo-Saxons soon replaced the Romans as the dominant force in the region.

The Angles moved in first and reclaimed areas of the former settlement that had been flooded, and eventually it would become the capital of the Kingdom of Northumbria. St. Paulinus came to York and became its first bishop, leading to the construction of the first Minster in 627, a precursor to the York Minster. York continued to grow as an economic, religious, and educational center well into the 9th century before the next invaders arrived—the Vikings. York also served as their capital, and they enlarged it even further than the Anglo-Saxons had. They named it Jórvík, which became anglicized to Yorvik, later shortened to York.

With the death of Eric Bloodaxe in 954, Northumbria fell under the control of the Anglo-Saxons once again, though it was still heavily influenced by Viking culture. Northumbria enjoyed relative autonomy until William the Conqueror brought York under his control during the Harrying of the North in 1069. He built castles and fought to keep control of the city. With North and South firmly united under a Norman king, York continued to grow and prosper during the medieval period, marred only by a massacre of the city's Jewish population in 1190 and the coming of the Black Death in 1349. The latter event is believed to have resulted in the deaths of half of York's population.

York managed to recover and continued to grow in its economic and political influence. By the time of the English Civil War, it became the center of King Charles I's court for six months in 1642 after the Parliamentarians caused him to flee London. Seen as a Royalist stronghold, York eventually fell to Cromwell's force in 1644. By the 1700s, York was the third-largest city in England after London and Norwich. Unfortunately, this was not to last, as the coming Industrial Revolution of the late $18^{th}$ and early $19^{th}$ centuries failed to take root in York, and other English cities soon out paced it in size and influence.

With the coming of the railway in 1839, rail carriage repair and construction soon took off as an industry, and York returned to prominence. Further progress was made in the $19^{th}$ century with the introduction of plumbing, gas lighting, public transportation, and the city's own police force. An 1825 Act of Parliament created the Improvement Commissioners, who were responsible for the lighting, paving, and cleaning of city streets. It proved to be quite necessary as the influx of Irish immigrants fleeing the Great Potato Famine resulted in them being forced into quickly built and often overcrowded slums, leading to several outbreaks of disease until their living conditions were improved.

York continued to grow at a rapid pace well into the early $20^{th}$ century, and it upgraded with better public utilities, including electric lights. The city also discovered its sweet tooth as confectionary industries such as Rowntree, Terry's, Fry, and Cadbury turned the city into a Mecca for chocolate lovers. Of course, these weren't the only industries still in York, and the city drew attention from Luftwaffe bombers during World War

II. Reconstruction began in 1945 and continued through 1960 as many Council houses were built and important city locations such as the Guildhall were restored.

On our one morning in York, we ended up sleeping in a bit and then had a great breakfast in the hotel. We had one goal for the day, which was to explore York. We checked out of the hotel and had them hold our bags and car so we could explore on foot.

It was raining again. But we had our brollies, so we made the wet walk over to York Minster. It was not far from our hotel, and it was nice to get out and stretch our legs a bit before getting back in the car for the day.

York Minster was simply amazing. Pretty much every cathedral we visit is amazing, but York Minster is very special. Its size dwarfs anything else in the city. It dominates all the views. Inside it's just as incredible, though we had the unwelcome guest of scaffolding on the inside (it's probably gone by now).

It's unknown when exactly Christianity came to York, but the summoning of a bishop from York to the Council of Arles suggests that faith has been an important part of the area since at least 312 AD. The first known church didn't arrive for nearly 300 years when one was built for the primary purpose of baptizing King Edwin of Northumbria in 627. That church was replaced with a more permanent stone structure, but it didn't last a century before it started falling apart.

Another church replaced that, which was joined by the addition of a school and a library. A fire then destroyed it, and its Saxon replacement was said to have 30 altars. As York was subject to repeated invasions for the next 300 years, records aren't very well kept from this period until the 11th century. After that church was destroyed by the Danes in 1080, the Norman Archbishop had it rebuilt in the Norman style, and that would be the cathedral that stood until the construction of the current abbey church.

Around 1215, Archbishop Walter de Gray wanted a Gothic cathedral built similar to the one at Canterbury. Construction started on the new cathedral in 1120 and took another 250 years to complete. The first parts were built where the north and south transepts finished in the 1250s. A central tower was constructed around the same time as the transepts, but it collapsed in 1407 and had to be rebuilt. The Charter House was started 10 years later and was finished around 1296. The nave was constructed starting in the 1280s based on the Norman foundation, and then work moved out to the eastern arm and the chapels. The outer roof was finished in 1330, but it would be another 30 years before the vaulting was done. The choir was the last part of the Norman church that was demolished in the 1390s. Since construction was completed, York Minster Abbey is actually the second-largest Gothic cathedral in Northern Europe, with an interior that is nearly 6,000 square meters.

Why the strange name? York Minster? And don't you dare call it a cathedral (I have gotten letters!). Well, the official name of York Minster Abbey is The Cathedral and Metropolitical Church of St. Peter at York. Since it was built before the Norman Conquest, after which the term "cathedral" began to see wide use, it is not named as a cathedral even though it technically is one and looks like one. But, like its sister Westminster Abbey, it's not a cathedral, even though, in practical reality, it is one.

The next big moment for York Minster Abbey came in the 1530s with the Dissolution of the Monasteries and the Crown raiding Catholic churches across the country for their riches as King Henry VIII transitioned to Anglicanism. The Catholic Queen Mary attempted to restore the damage done under her father's reign, but her efforts were then undone during the reign of Elizabeth I, who attempted to rid Anglican churches of any Catholic imagery. During the English Civil War, it appeared that further damage could be wrought by the forces of Oliver Cromwell when they captured York, but Ferdinando and Thomas Fairfax worked to protect the cathedral's treasures from further damage and have a plaque in York Minster dedicated to their efforts.

You can see the results of the Reformation today when you visit the place. While beautiful, the interiors are stark in their plainness. It's a bit sad to think that while the stonework is beautiful and on fine display, centuries earlier it would have been covered in painting and imagery. Now, the only imagery you have is the stained glass, which is some of the most beautiful I've ever seen.

Over the 18th and 19th centuries the cathedral underwent some of its first major restorations and some setbacks. The floor of the entire church was re-laid in marble from 1730 to 1737, and a major restoration began in 1802. Then a fire caused by arsonist Jonathan Martin damaged the east arm of York Minster in 1829, and another fire (accidental this time) left the southwest tower and south aisle charred shells. Compounding York Minster's troubles, the church went into debt in the 1850s but was saved through the work of Augustus Duncombe.

The 20th century produced many memorable moments for York Minster Abbey. In 1972 excavations done during work to reinforce the foundation uncovered a Roman Principia which is now part of an exhibit. 1984 saw another fire, and the heat was intense enough to shatter the stained glass in the rose window, but fortunately, it held together and was able to be restored. Within the last few years York Minster Abbey went through another restoration at a cost of £23 million.

We took our time walking around and soaked in the atmosphere. It was not very crowded, which was nice. York Minster is now the official cathedral for the Royal Air Force, so there were soldiers inside preparing for an RAF100-related service. The choir was rehearsing, and it was sublimely beautiful. At one point, we just sat down and enjoyed being present in the moment.

We wandered around the whole place. We went into the octagonal Chapter House. While the cathedral is enough to make your mouth drop open, the York Minster Chapter House is one of the most incredible spaces I have ever been in.

After we left the cathedral, we had a wander around York, exploring the narrow side streets, many closed off from traffic. York is a ridiculously wonderful walkable small city. We browsed the shops – I found a lovely topsy-turvy bookstore. By this point, it was approaching lunchtime, so we stopped to eat in one of the many restaurants in York.

After lunch, we had a wander around some more to find The Shambles, the famous narrow street that's been featured in pictures of York for years. We were a bit let down by it, to be honest. It was beautiful, but it was packed with fellow tourists. We struggled to walk through it. I couldn't get any decent pictures of the place. I also found the proliferation of Harry Potter themed shops all selling the same things rather dismaying. It felt very Disneyfied. Look, I get that it looks like a real-life Diagon Alley, but turning one of the most unique streets in Britain into a tourist trap is rather annoying. None of the stuff you can buy there is unique or interesting; it is all the same Harry Potter tat you can get anywhere these days. Oh well. Still, there are plenty of non-Harry Potter shops and tearooms to enjoy. It's still worth seeing. I highly recommend visiting on market day, as it adds a bit more bustle to the scene.

I'm also happy to report that York has some very lovely second-hand bookshops, the kind that are rabbit warrens of books that you can barely navigate around. You know, the best kind of little British bookstores. We were traveling light, so I had to resist the urge to fill a second suitcase with books, especially since we were planning a visit to a very special bookstore the next day.

York's major selling point is how walkable it is. You can visit all the major tourist attractions on foot, and it's not unpleasant, even in the rain. If it hadn't been raining, we probably would have done a boat ride or explored more of the narrow medieval streets. Walking the circuit of the medieval city walls would have to wait for another visit. It was late, and we needed to hit the road. After York, every mile of the road we traveled would be a mile that would be new for us.

How exciting!

*Jonathan Thomas*

# CHAPTER SEVENTEEN
## RUINED ABBEYS

If I had to pick the one heritage entity I love most in the British landscape, it would be ruined abbeys. I am not a religious man for various reasons. Yet, I find myself completely in love with ruined abbeys. Not because they are a physical representation of the failures of religion but because they're beautiful. Every single one that I've visited over the years has this FEELING. It's hard to describe, but I'll do my best. I knew that when we planned our route for this drive, I'd just have to include a ruined abbey or two. The one we did end up visiting ended up being one that wasn't on the itinerary, and we just happened to be passing. Fountains Abbey is one of the most incredible abbey ruins I've been to.

The world that built these abbeys is practically an alien world. It's unrecognizable to us. The world was in anarchy. It's often called 'the Dark Ages,' but that's really an unfair characterization. But, at least in England, this time period was a time of instability, strife, and poverty. England was a place that was fought over constantly after the Romans left. If anything, the abbeys that were founded when Britain was converted to Christianity brought stability, society, and civilization to a wild place.

Where governance failed in medieval England, where local landlords, earls, princes, and kings merely saw their kingdoms as property to be exploited, the churches stepped in to provide some societal structure. Each abbey was a pocket of civilization in Britain, with a focus on worship and service to God. Each one was a community that did not live in isolation; there were thriving towns and villages around them that sprouted up to support them. Some of them turned into major cities, some fell to ruin. While they were 'alive,' they were pockets of civilization in a world of chaos.

Driving up the A1(M) through Yorkshire, we saw the signs for Fountains Abbey. We decided to stop primarily for National Trust tea and cake. The ruined abbey was a bonus for us. Serendipity was going to lead us there. What's always surprising about detours like this is how far away they end up being from the main roads. The signs made it seem like Fountains Abbey was nearby. In reality, it was almost a half hour away from the motorway, down increasingly narrowing lanes the further and further away you got from civilization.

Fountains Abbey exists because of sheep but it started, as these things do, with a disagreement amongst some men.

The settlement at Fountains Abbey got its start with a dispute between Benedictine monks in Yorkshire. Thirteen of the monks from the abbey at St. Mary's left in 1132 over disagreements with their brothers, namely that the Benedictines there lived an extravagant and ungodly lifestyle. Preferring a more devout and less frivolous form of service to God, they formed a Cistercian order with the blessings of Thurston, the Archbishop of York, who also gave them land in the valley of the River Skell. The valley had plenty of resources that the monks used to build the first stone church and several wooden buildings, which would be replaced in 1143 after the election of Henry Murdac as Abbot.

The buildings ended up being replaced due to an attack on the abbey in 1146 by a mob angry at Murdac for opposing the election of William Fitzherbert as Archbishop of York burned down the two-story stone church and other wooden buildings. The new church that would form the basis of the abbey was constructed starting not long after the attack and was completed in 1170. As the abbey grew in size, it also grew in wealth and influence. While the monks focused on their responsibilities to God, they brought in lay brothers for the tasks of maintaining the abbey, which included sheep farming. It was from the sheep that Fountains Abbey acquired most of its wealth, and Fountains, at its height, was the largest producer of Cistercian wool in England. Some historians estimate that in 1300, Fountains Abbey produced 76 sacks of wool and was home to roughly 18,000 sheep.

Unfortunately, this wealth was not to last. Over the next century, Fountains Abbey was hit by Black Death, attacks from the Scots, bad harvests, and sheep disease. Many of the lay brothers left, and sheep farming progressively changed to dairy farming. Fountains managed to bounce back from this disaster to become as wealthy as ever, which unfortunately attracted the attention of King Henry VIII during the Dissolution of the Monasteries.

During the English Reformation, which was primarily started by Henry's desire to divorce his wife and father a son with a new wife, he spotted an opportunity to seize wealth. Wealth beyond what most people could imagine. The church in England was extremely powerful and wealthy, with dozens of abbeys spread out all over the country, which owned hundreds of thousands of acres of land. While the abbeys were dedicated to their religious missions, they were also landlords and businesses that held considerable wealth and power.

Tyrants do not share power well.

What followed was one of the biggest transfers of wealth in world history (probably not surpassed until the Soviet Union was formed).

As befell many great church institutions throughout Great Britain, Fountains Abbey could not escape the Dissolution of the Monasteries that began in 1539. The abbey was closed by order of the Crown, which seized the Cistercian order's land, buildings, and wealth. In 1540, the Crown sold the land and buildings to Sir Richard Gresham. The monks and their flock were pensioned off, and the abbey became the property of someone who had other intentions for it.

The property that contained Fountains Abbey continued to pass down to Sir Richard's descendants. Like many monastic buildings that were not repurposed by the Church of England, much of its wood, stone, metal roof, and other resources were appropriated for other nearby buildings. If you want to see where the ruins of Fountains Abbey ended up, you only need to look at the surrounding landscape. Bits of it are everywhere.

One of the buildings for which Fountain Abbey's stone would be repurposed was Fountains Hall. In 1597, the Gresham family sold the Fountains property to Stephen Proctor, who used stone from the ruins to construct the Hall starting in 1598. Completed in 1604, Fountains Hall is a beautiful example of an Elizabethan prodigy house, which was largely built for the owner to show off their wealth. After Proctor died, the home passed to the Messenger family, who in turn sold it to William Aislabe in the 18th century as part of a legal settlement. The Aislabes built the Studley Royal Water Garden on the Fountains Abbey property, which is one of the best examples of a water garden in the United Kingdom.

As the attentions of the Crown and the new property owner turned elsewhere, the abbey began to fall into ruin. It does not take long for places like this to become a shell of their former selves.

One of the reasons that the Aislabes had sought the Fountains Abbey property was for its romantic attraction. The world was suddenly in love with ruins. It found their crumbling mass, often covered in vines and overgrown weeds, to be romantic in its own right. And if it happened to be sitting in a pretty landscape, all the better. Something could be romantic simply for being… romantic.

The art and poetry of the late 18th century was dominated by Romanticism, which not only put an emphasis on emotion and individualism but sought to praise nature and history, often as a nostalgic reaction to the Industrial Revolution. It thus became fashionable for the wealthy to have ruins on their property and, despite the pilfering of its stone and fixtures over the centuries, Fountains Abbey was still one of the most complete Medieval churches in England.

Along with the imminently wealthy visitors to Studley Royal, the ruins of Fountains Abbey attracted a number of Romantic artists, writers, and poets. The ruins have been the subject of watercolors by Samuel Hieronymus Grimm, pencil drawings by George Cuitt Junior, and oil paintings by J.W.M. Turner. Poet Letitia Elizabeth Landon wrote about Fountains Abbey at least twice during her career with Fountains Abbey and The Fairy of the Fountains.

The entire place, the ruins and the Studley Royal gardens, are now in the masterful care of the National Trust. They've built a suitably impressive visitors' center, which is what you come to expect from these places these days. There was ample tea and cake.

While we stopped primarily for the ruin, we decided to have tea and cake first.

Priorities, am I right?

I'm very glad we did, and it was everything we hoped it would be. I didn't realize it at the time, but it would be our last National Trust tea and cake of the trip (and my last for four years). I can still taste my brownie and tea. I longed for it in my absence from Britain.

The ruins are a bit of a trek from the visitors' center, which has been carefully placed in the landscape to blend in. As a consequence, you have to walk to it. But it's an easy walk, and there's often nothing more lovely than a stroll through a National Trust parkland - even if there are spotty rain showers (always bring an umbrella when traveling in Britain). There was a neat little exhibit on the wool that used to be produced there and a chance to knit your contribution into the communal scarf that was several meters long at that point. As an avid knitter, Jackie loved putting her stamp on such a long-term project.

As you approach, what strikes you most of all is how intact the place still is. For a ruin, there is quite a bit of it still there. Some ruins I've been to, you can't really tell what's left (like the ruins of Shaftesbury Abbey - not recognizably a ruin). This one, if you closed your eyes, still looks like it is a thriving community. Much of the main tower is still there, as are a lot of the vaulted cellarium (which is just incredibly, delightfully, endless).

The place is MASSIVE.

It's hard to convey the scale of the place in words - but you can see why this was one of the wealthiest places in Britain and why Henry VIII coveted it so much. The surrounding grounds are lush and green, you can hear the nearby river Skell. The green grass goes right up to the ruins themselves as if they sprouted from the ground.

Massive arches surround you in what's left of the nave - they tower above you almost like skyscrapers. How they were built in such a 'primitive' time boggles the mind. How they're still standing with so little support is a miracle on its own. The National Trust takes good care of the place. While the Victorians loved how romantic the places were, covered in trees and weeds, unfortunately that causes more damage than anything. The Trust keeps the stones nice and clean now, which helps preserve the ruins in their current state. They call it 'arrested decay.' It slows the wasting down; one day, these stones will all be on the ground. One day they will be covered in grass. One day the sun will stop burning. Nothing escapes the ravages of time.

Which is why it's even more of a privilege to visit special places like this.

We had the site largely to ourselves, which is the best way to experience a place like this.

It is the most amazing ruin I have ever visited. Even now, four years later, I'm trying to figure out a way to fit a quick visit to it on another trip I'm planning.

The modern British live amongst the ruins of former civilizations, and it's incredible. Most places have a local ruin or castle or stately home. When you come from a place that has none of these, you appreciate special places like this all the more. Stand in the ruins. Listen to the wind. If you listen

closely, you can hear the voices of those that came before.
    And sheep.
    You'll probably hear sheep.

## A World Heritage Site

Fountains Abbey & Studley Royal is one of just two World Heritage Sites in Yorkshire, and the National Trust looks after 8 places in the UK on the World Heritage Site list.

World Heritage Sites are places considered by the United Nations Educational, Scientific and Cultural Organisation (UNESCO) to be of outstanding universal value to mankind.

World Heritage Sites belong to all the peoples of the world, irrespective of where they are located. By identifying these special places of great cultural and/or natural value UNESCO aims to safeguard these places so that they can be passed to future generations.

There are currently 28 World Heritage Sites in the UK. They range from the iconic Tower of London to Titus Salt's philanthropic vision at Salt's Mill and Saltaire village, impressive Stonehenge to Liverpool docklands' maritime city, dramatic Giant's Causeway to Edinburgh's medieval old town and elegant Georgian new town.

# CHAPTER EIGHTEEN
## The National Trust

A social worker, a lawyer, and a priest walk into a pub....
It sounds like a joke, but actually I'm talking about the founders of the National Trust. When we visited Fountains Abbey, I didn't know it would be the last time I visited a National Trust property for many years. It was the perfect National Trust experience and suitable for a last visit. Thinking about it reminds me of my particular love of the institution. Many Americans may not be familiar with it, but they need to be.

An aspect of the drive I was really looking forward to was visiting several National Trust properties along the way (and which helped is decide our route). Each one is a unique experience, but also an experience where you expect to find similarities. Most of the major properties have gardens, a tearoom, gift shop, and even sometimes a second-hand bookshop. I do love a good second-hand bookshop. I've visited dozens of National Trust properties over the years. They are always the highlight of our travels. In fact, the National Trust is one of the greatest things Britain has ever devised.

Without the existence of the National Trust, it is unlikely that England would today be recognizably 'England.' The Trust was founded in 1895 to preserve both open spaces and properties of historical, cultural, or natural interest. It grew out of a desire to prevent the unchecked spread of industrialization and development across a landscape steeped in history and populated with buildings reaching back into the roots of the country. By making it possible for stately homes to be donated to the Trust, instead of sold to pay death duties, hundreds of properties were preserved for the enjoyment of English and overseas visitors alike. National Trust properties are a touchstone of earlier times, and the extensive countryside holdings of the Trust preserve the unique character of the English landscape.

Like several other quintessentially British institutions, The National Trust was born of 'foreign' influences, in this case in the mind of the American landscape architect Charles Eliot. Eliot was a lover of natural beauty and thus an instinctive Romantic who, in 1890, began a campaign to preserve a virgin stand of trees in Belmont, Massachusetts. His campaign led to a conference at MIT with broader aims to acquire, hold, protect, and administer, for the benefit of the public, beautiful and historical places. The state of Massachusetts passed legislation creating The Trustees of Reservations in 1891 to achieve that goal. That organization continues its work today.

Meanwhile, in England, social reformers interested in improving the miserable lives of the poor had been influenced by John Ruskin to consider the place of natural beauty in a full life. Ruskin was the pre-eminent art and social critic of the second half of the 19<sup>th</sup> century, writing prolifically on a wide range of subjects. Today he is considered an early environmentalist, and he not only believed that art should be taken from nature but that everyone had the right to access to nature – a very relevant social concern when many lived and died in dirty industrial cities.

Influenced by Ruskin, and under the slogan Bring Beauty Home to the Poor, the campaigner for improved urban living standards, Octavia Hill, and her sister Miranda, founded the Kyrle Society in 1875 to bring art and open spaces to the poor. The society's Open Spaces Committee successfully protected Hampstead Heath and Parliament Hill Fields from development. Working with the Hill sisters on the campaign to protect Hampstead Heath was a solicitor, Robert Hunter. At the age of 22, Hunter had won an essay contest supporting 'common rights to land' – a principle dating back to medieval times that gave residents of an area certain rights, such as grazing and firewood gathering, on land to which they had no legal title. He extended that idea to the right of people to 'health, comfort and convenience' of land around urban areas. His work provided an important legal argument for the preservation of open spaces and by 1875 most of his concepts were enshrined in law.

A final key figure was Canon Hardwicke Rawnsley, a Lake District clergyman and life-long friend of Beatrix Potter. He had gained the assistance of Robert Hunter in preventing the construction of an industrial railway in the Lake District. These activists enjoyed wide support from a host of influential figures, from Ruskin to William Morris, as well as Lord Tennyson, John Stuart Mills, and countless others. The rapid expansion of urbanization was seen as a major threat to the English countryside, and there was a strong feeling that the 'dark, satanic mills' must not prevail.

The trio of Rawnsley, Hunter, and Octavia Hill took inspiration from Charles Eliot's success in Massachusetts and formed the National Trust for Places of Historic Interest or Natural Beauty on the 12th of January 1895. In 1877 William Morris and others had established an organization with similar aims, although more focused on architecture, called the Society for the Protection of Ancient Buildings. Morris's main concern was the extensive 'restoration' of older buildings by removing later additions to create an idealized original state. He believed that a building should be preserved as a cultural record, not restored or, as he put it, 'forged.'

The first opportunity for Morris to put his ideas into practice came when he was approached by a London architect, Owen Fleming, for advice on the restoration of Alfriston Clergy House. This was a 14th century building in East Sussex owned by the Church of England. Fleming had been contacted by the new vicar, Reverend F.W. Beynon, for advice on restoring the derelict building still occupied by an elderly lady. Due to a lack of funds, Beynon asked Morris for advice, and Morris put him in touch with a fellow clergyman - Canon Rawnsley. He, of course, passed the matter to the National Trust. Octavia Hill and Morris shared a common concern with 'restoration' and agreed instead that the building would simply be 'preserved from decay,' making it structurally sound but changing as little as possible. This distinction became a founding principle of the National Trust and still inspires almost all their activities. Architects trained by the Society for the Protection of Ancient Buildings preserved many National Trust properties, continuing to avoid 'restoration.'

The Clergy House was duly purchased from the Church for £10 and carefully preserved by the Arts & Crafts architect and designer Alfred Hoare Powell. This became the first National Trust property and also perhaps the inspiration for the 'oak leaf' emblem of the Trust, taken from a wood carving on a cornice of the building. The Trust's first nature reserve was Wicken Fen, a wetland in Cambridgeshire, donated by Charles Rothschild in 1901, and its first archaeological monument was White Barrow, a Neolithic barrow in Wiltshire, purchased in 1907.

The National Trust Act of 1907, an act of Parliament, established a legal basis for the Trust to acquire property as a non-profit society and established its aims as:

> The preservation for the benefit of the Nation of lands and tenements (including buildings) of beauty or historic interest and, as regards lands, for the preservation of their natural aspect, features, and animal and plant life. Also, the preservation of furniture, pictures, and chattels of any description having national and historic, or artistic interest.

Several other Acts followed over the years as the Trust grew. The Trust operated chiefly by encouraging - and getting - donations of property from the owners, although some properties were also purchased with funds from financial donations. A major period of growth occurred between 1924 and 1931 under the chairmanship of John Bailey, a literary critic and lecturer. He was able to encourage many donations of houses and land to the Trust, using a combination of persuasion and enthusiasm. Beatrix Potter donated her extensive properties in the Lake District to the Trust upon her death in 1943.

The formation of the National Trust coincided with the introduction of Inheritance Taxes in 1894. The rate of tax increased steadily throughout most of the 20th century, with a large jump in 1945 following the election of a Labour government under Clement Attlee. For the inheritors of large estates, rich in heritage but poor in cash, paying these duties often involved breaking up estates and selling homes. The National Trust offered another way, where descendants could give the property to the Trust in lieu of these death duties but continue to live in the home for life. This brought many country homes under the care of the Trust and accounted for the growing attention given to homes over land that occurred during the 20th century. In 1967 this focus was challenged by members, and a new, region-based structure was developed to encourage more diverse activity. Today the Trust usually requires an endowment for maintenance to accompany donations of houses unless they are of extreme cultural value. It has also expanded its collections with such entities as the childhood terrace homes of Paul McCartney and John Lennon.

The National Trust today owns over 500 historic houses, gardens and monuments, that are open to the public. It owns 610,000 acres, mostly of the countryside (1.5% of Britain), including 1/5 of the coastline and large parts of the Lake District and the Peak District National Park. The sale or mortgage of Trust land is inalienable, and any sale would require a new Act of Parliament, and the Trust also has the power to make by-laws regulating the use of its land. The Scottish National Trust carries out similar work in Scotland.

What a remarkable organization this is. We simply don't have an equivalent here in the USA. Many historic buildings get easily swept away in the name of progress, despite campaign groups who try to save them. For a building to be saved, there has to be private money willing to save it (and let's face it, this money has to come from a rich benefactor who's interested in saving something). Things don't get saved because of their importance and should be saved.

The National Trust motto is 'Forever, for everyone,' which to me is one of the most beautiful official I've ever come across. Their mission is simple: protect a thing forever for the enjoyment of everyone. It's no wonder that the National Trust is one of Britain's most cherished institutions (and thankfully resists the urge to participate in 'culture wars' that try to change it). Like the BBC, the National Trust is an institution that some forces would be perfectly happy to see go away (like property developers), but Britain would be a much poorer place if it ever did.

It can't.

Because Parliament said so.

Titles are forever and can never be sold.

Pretty stately homes, miles of coast, crumbling cottages, they belong to the British people, forever, for everyone.

# CHAPTER NINETEEN
## Durham

We drove on to Durham from Fountains Abbey, not a long journey. After brief rain, the sun stayed out for us. Our destination was the Hotel Indigo, which is just over the river from all the main attractions in Durham. We arrived too late to do any sightseeing, so we opted to get settled in, catch up on business and then eat dinner at the hotel. It was very nice, an old university building converted into a hotel but done so that the building's original features were still visible.

The Hotel Indigo is a stunning architectural marvel. Located in the former Old Shire Building, this hotel is a true testament to Durham's rich history and heritage. Built in the early 18th century, the Old Shire Building was originally used as a jail and courthouse. Over time, it served various purposes, including as a library and a registry office.

The building was eventually converted into a hotel, and

given a new lease on life. The lush interiors were preserved and restored to their former glory, and they are most impressive. The hotel has been decorated in a contemporary style that blends seamlessly with the building's historic architecture. The result is a space that is both elegant and cozy, with an atmosphere that is truly unique. I was particularly taken by the ornate tiling located in all the common areas; it all feels a bit too beautiful for a provincial hotel – so it was quite something to experience in person.

The restaurant we ate in was an old university chamber, and it was one of the most beautiful I've ever been to. We dined under the most magnificent ornate dome. The food was great too – it was apparently a famous celebrity chef's restaurant (Marco Pierre White). The restaurant was filled with teenagers in town for touring Durham University and dining with their parents.

The next day we were able to explore Durham properly. I was very happy to be there. Durham is not a traditional stop on the Land's End to John o' Groats tour. Most routes on LeJog take the western route through England. It's something we added in, mostly because I discovered that some of my ancestors came from there, and we wanted to find where they lived (this was covered in my previous book Adventures in Anglotopia, so I will not rehash it here).

One of my favorite writers, Bill Bryson, once wrote in his bestselling book Notes from a Small Island that Durham was the most perfect English city. The city was so grateful that he did so that the University of Durham made him Honorary Chancellor, a position he accepted with aplomb.

Durham, like Oxford, Cambridge, and St Andrews, has been a center of learning in Britain for centuries. Its university is one of the best in Britain, and often students will opt to go here instead of going through the rigors of getting into Oxford or Cambridge. During our time there it was 'visit week' when prospective students descend on the city to check out the university and decide if it is the right place for them. During our dinner that first night there were quite a few bookish-looking teens dining with a parent. All were excited and eager to explore the city.

There was a palpable excitement in the air, and it added color to our visit.

Durham is a pretty medieval city situated along a picturesque river, and the city is most famous for its cathedral, which would be our primary destination for the day.

Durham Cathedral is a place that is multi-faceted, holding many roles over hundreds of years of history, from a place of worship to a school for witchcraft and wizardry. The cathedral's own history touches on every era in British antiquity, from the Norman Conquest to the English Civil War and into the 21$^{st}$ century.

The ecclesiastical history of Durham has its origins in the Diocese of Lindisfarne. In 875 AD monks from Lindisfarne fled the area after repeated Viking raids, taking the relics of St. Cuthbert with them. They moved about six miles north of Durham's present location, but further raids caused them to move again in 995. According to legend, the monks followed a couple of milkmaids searching for a dun-colored cow, and when they reached a peninsula on the River Wear, Cuthbert's coffin became immovable. The monks took it as a sign that this was where they were meant to settle, and their new church became the foundation of the City of Durham.

In 1080, after the Norman Conquest, King William I appointed William de St. Calais as the first Prince-Bishop of Durham, the title reflecting William's dual role as a religious and secular leader. The Prince-Bishop was not only the head of the church at Durham but also the Earl of Northumbria. Bishop William felt a grander building was necessary for Cuthbert's remains and demolished the Anglo-Saxon White Church to make way for the construction of Durham Cathedral.

Construction began in 1093, and the design is a fine example of Romanesque architecture that was common to the Normans. By the time of Bishop William's death in 1096, the Chapter House was far enough along that he was able to be buried in it. Bishop Ranaulf Flambard took over, and work continued on the Chapter House, which was finished around 1140. Flambard was succeeded in the 1170s by Hugh de Puiset, who led the construction of the Galilee Chapel, where the Venerable Bede was buried.

The Venerable Bede is an interesting character, and when you understand him you understand how Durham, a remote city in the far north of England, could become a center of learning. Bede is most famous for having written the Ecclesiastical History of the English People, and he's considered the father of English history writing. Written in 731 AD it's a dense history of the Christian Churches in England and of England in general; its main focus is on the conflict between the pre-Schism Roman Rite and Celtic Christianity. It was originally composed in Latin and is considered one of the most important original references on Anglo-Saxon history and has played a key role in the development of an English national identity. It is believed to have been completed in 731 when Bede was approximately 59 years old. While modern historians have questioned the accuracy of many of Bede's assertions, it's still considered an important document of early English history before the Norman invasion.

To this day, many historians and students of history will

visit Durham Cathedral just to pay homage to his grave (which is at the entrance to the Cathedral and not in it properly).

The Benedictine monks continued to look after Durham Cathedral until the Dissolution of the Monasteries. In 1538, King Henry VIII ordered the tomb of St. Cuthbert destroyed, and the cathedral's assets seized for the Crown. Hugh Whitehead was the last Prior of the monastery when it was dissolved in 1540 and was appointed by Henry as the cathedral's first Dean, with 12 of his former monks serving as his Canons, forming the cathedral's Anglican administration. Cuthbert was reburied in a simple slab that became worn from the knees of pilgrims who continued to visit the site. Unfortunately, many artifacts and furnishings did not survive the Reformation as they were destroyed in favor of the new Anglican doctrine. Despite all this, the cathedral did not become a ruin like so many others in Northern England. It continued to play an important role in the new Church of England.

That sets Durham Cathedral apart from its counterparts in the North of England as it wasn't ruined like Fountains instead it became the center of a great university. That and the cathedral still retains much of its Norman characteristics. They were not covered over by future generations' renovations, or whitewashed during the Protestant Reformation like so many ecclesiastical decorations in Britain. Bill Bryson said that Durham Cathedral "like all great buildings of antiquity, is essentially just a giant pile of rubble held in place by two thin layers of dressed stone." And he is absolutely right. The building feels old.

Once we entered and paid our admission, we hurried to explore. Sadly, and forgive me if I rant a bit here, the place did not allow photography inside, which is a shame because the interiors are incredible. I understand why places like this don't allow photography, but I don't have to like it. Taking photos of special places in Britain is my bread and butter as a publisher putting out a website (and previously a magazine). I need pictures. And I have absolutely no good pictures of my own of the interior because I was expressly forbidden from taking them. The stonework on the Norman arches is quite something to behold. This place is one of England's finest treasures.

Though, the bonus, I suppose, of not being able to take any pictures was that I had to put my camera away and experience the place completely with my own eyes and not through the eyepiece of my camera. I suppose I should be grateful for that.

So, forced to put the camera away and inhabit the space rather than try to capture it, we slowly made our way through the cathedral, taking our time to take in the ancient, sacral space that is still used for its primary purpose. All around you are elements from the various ages of Britain - most notably the Norman details on the columns and arches. It's very dark inside, which wasn't helped by it being a particularly cloudy day.

I was struck by the sheer size and grandeur of the space, as I usually am in cathedrals like this. The soaring, vaulted ceilings gave the impression of infinite space, while the stone carvings and elaborate stained glass windows added a sense of intricate detail to the overall design.

As I walked through the nave, I was impressed by the intricacy and precision of the stonework. The pointed arches and ribbed vaults of the Gothic architecture gave the space a sense of verticality, while the intricate carvings that adorned the columns and capitals added a sense of whimsy and playfulness. And this was true Gothic architecture, not any of that Victorian copying.

The choir area was particularly impressive, with its ornately carved stalls and soaring Gothic vaults. The choir screen, with its intricate tracery and delicate carvings, was a true masterpiece in the Gothic style.

The stained-glass windows were another highlight of the cathedral's interior. The intricate designs and bold colors of the windows added a sense of vibrancy and life to the space, while the play of light and shadow across the interior created a sense of drama and depth. However, this was a bit muted on a cloudy day.

As always, it was a treat to inhabit such a space for a short period of time. I just wish I'd gotten a few pictures!

After we left the cathedral, we wandered around central Durham. The city was very busy, humming with prospective students and their parents. The shops were swamped with people buying Durham University swag, but I still managed to pick up a few books that looked interesting. Jackie needed a new pair of shoes, and we found a shop that had an affordable selection of shoes (yes, she did not pack a suitable pair of shoes for walking, it's never too late to make a course correction in the footwear department).

I quite liked Durham, and Bill Bryson was definitely right. It is a perfect little English city. We will have to return another day when we have more time. I was rather jealous of all the young students getting ready to study there - their whole lives ahead of them, dreams of learning fresh and exciting. That's how Durham feels, and that's nice.

# CHAPTER NINETEEN
## Barter Books

We arrived in Alnwick late in the day and stumbled into a town in the middle of a food festival. The town was heaving. The intention had always been to visit Barter Books, one of the most famous bookstores in Britain - for two reasons - first is that it was a beautiful old place located in an abandoned and restored railway station. That alone was enough to make the place famous. But then, a few years ago, a rare poster was found that led to one of the biggest non-Internet 'memes' the world has seen, Keep Calm and Carry On.

The car park for Barter books was full and cramped. We had trouble navigating it with our stupidly large vehicle. We drove around it as best we could and just could not find a space. We slowly backed our way out of the car park, snarling traffic along the way, safe in the feeling that we weren't from around these parts.

Plan B was needed.

We drove around the block and found several streets of beautiful, terraced houses. There was plenty of space there and, with no signage to indicate we couldn't park there, we did so and then walked a short way back to Barter Books.

Finally, I was making a pilgrimage that I'd wanted to make for years.

Barter Books is so much more than just a bookshop, it's a temple to used and new literature, and it comes with a special history (and a few surprises) all its own. Barter Books is a place that goes back in time not only for its contents but the building itself, conjuring up relics of long ago and transforming them into a part of our popular culture. It's a perfect encapsulation of the British attitude to old and unloved things that find a brilliant second life.

Well before Stuart and Mary Manley opened the bookshop in 1991, their building took people to very different realms. This Victorian railway station was designed by William Bell and opened in 1887. For what was a small market town at the time, Alnwick Railway Station's 32,000 square feet were enormous and stately. Part of the reason for this was that Alnwick was the seat of the Duke of Northumberland, so the rail station had to be grand enough to impress visiting royalty. In 1968, as part of a profitability scheme for the failing British Rail proposed by Richard Beeching, the branch line was closed, and the rail station fell into disuse. Its heyday had not lasted long, and it risked being abandoned for longer than it was ever a train station.

Royal visits, however, were common before it closed. Queen Victoria certainly had reason to visit Alnwick during her reign, as her governess was Charlotte Florentia Percy, the wife of the 3rd Duke of Northumberland, Hugh Percy. The Percy family still owns the castle, and portions of it are used as their private residence. The last monarch to visit the castle was Queen Elizabeth II in 2011. We'd hoped to visit the castle that day, the Harry Potter fan in me was desperate to have a wander around the place.

The old railway station sat abandoned and unused until the Manleys bought the derelict building and converted it into a bookshop in the early 90s. Despite the new use, they wanted to make sure to harken back to the station's history. The entrance to Barter Books is found in the station's old parcel room, and the bars for the ticket agent are still there on the window. The store also takes up parts of the station's central island and outbound platform. There's even a little miniature train that runs above the heads of customers, as well as the old station clock that still keeps time. Of course, Barter Books has more to its interior than trains, and its interior design is something out of this world.

In the various rooms of Barter Books, you can find bright neon lights, hanging paper lanterns, important literary quotes, and even a life-size mural of 33 writers done by local artist Peter Dodd. The shop has plenty of comfy seating for you to lounge in while you peruse the wares to figure out what you're going to buy. Within the walls of the old station, you'll find an ice cream parlor built out of the station master's old office called Paradise. One of the best parts is the shop's café, the Station Buffet, which offers coffee, tea, sandwiches, and other edible delights. At one point, the shop staff managed to find a decades-old fern that had been kept alive due to a drippy faucet and a skylight in the ceiling.

We arrived at the bookshop hungry, so that buffet was the perfect spot for lunch. While the place was very busy, we managed to get our order in and find an empty table. Which leads to another wonderful piece of Barter's history—its secrets. Since the store opened in 1991, periodic construction projects have unearthed a fascinating number of discoveries. Part of what led to the creation of the Station Buffet was the uncovering of a room the Manleys didn't know existed when shop manager David Champion was looking for more office space. The food was yummy and filled our empty bellies. We had decided to eat before exploring the bookshop, since I knew that would take a long time as Barter Books estimates its catalog has over 45,000 books, and they sell roughly 3,000 books per week. When I went to the loo, I came across what made the bookshop a worldwide sensation, the original Keep Calm and Carry On poster, framed and mostly hidden on the way to the loo.

In 2000, Barter Books helped shape British pop culture after Stuart Manley discovered a Keep Calm and Carry On poster in a box of old books that had been purchased at auction. Mary Manley loved the poster and had it framed, hanging it up in the shop. The customers loved it too, and soon Barter Books began printing copies of it and other WWII posters to sell, beginning a trend that would eventually reach all parts of the globe.

Keep Calm and Carry On was one of three motivational posters printed by the British government for use in World War II to help boost morale. While the other two posters were widely distributed, KCCO had 2.5 million copies printed, but they were held in reserve for times of great crisis and never actually distributed. Historians knew the poster once existed, but it had been forgotten in general memory. Amazing how something reproduced could be forgotten. But the Keep Calm and Carry On trend hit the world at the perfect time. It was like a call from the past. It echoed Britain's 'stiff upper lip' – that, yes, things can get very bad indeed, but sunny days will return, so the only sensible thing to do is to keep calm and carry on with life. A cup of tea would also certainly help the situation.

It's a good message and one I've needed throughout my own life. So it was moving, in my own little way, to visit the place where the phrase was rediscovered. It's like paying homage to an old friend; long gone but not forgotten. The Keep Calm and Carry On craze is now out of fashion but the phrase and sentiment is timeless.

After lunch, it was showtime. Jackie and I separated, and we fanned out to get lost in this beautiful bookstore. It has a wonderful selection. Getting lost in the stacks of a secondhand British bookstore is one of my happy places. Knowing we still had much travel in front of us, I didn't want to weigh us down with too many books. So, I decided to be sensible and look for one book that I'd heard about but hadn't read yet - Cider with Rosie by Laurie Lee. I did manage to find a copy (and I'm so glad I did, I read the book after our return, and it is one of the finest books about England I've ever read - put this book down and go read it for yourself, I'll be here when you return). I also picked up a beautiful old map of Dorset, one of the old Bartholomew maps, colorful and full of detail you would not expect in such an old map.

Barter Books is really the dream of a perfect bookstore – a great selection with a rich history, located in an old building full of character. I could spend days there, perfectly content. It could be my entire life and, if I had to exist in some kind of inescapable purgatory, I would very much prefer it be this bookstore. Sadly, we spent too much time in the store and missed the opening times of Alnwick Castle. That's all right; it just gives us an excuse to return to this most wonderful of places.

    We returned to our car and resumed our journey northwards. What followed was an incredible drive along the main road that follows the northeastern coast of England. It's sublimely scenic. The endless blue and grey North Sea stretches along the infinite horizons. You're up on a bluff for parts of this drive, so you're far above the water and, as you gaze out, it's like looking at a million diamonds shimmering in the late afternoon sun. One of the most impressive sites was Bamburgh Castle, nestled on its own hill, almost surrounded by water.

    It is a stunning landmark located on the Northumberland coast. It is situated on top of a rocky outcrop overlooking the North Sea, providing stunning views of the surrounding landscape. The castle has a rich history dating back to the Anglo-Saxon period, and it has served as a royal residence, a military stronghold, and a museum. Today, Bamburgh Castle is one of the most important and iconic historical sites in England, attracting visitors from all over the world who come to marvel at its impressive architecture, learn about its fascinating history, and enjoy the breathtaking views of the Northumberland coast. Another location we would have to return to one day. One of my big takeaways from the whole journey is the seemingly obvious lesson that there is so much more to Britain that I haven't explored in 20 years of travel. I will spend the rest of my life trying to see it all. After several hours along the coast of the northern most bits of England, it was finally time to enter somewhere I have wanted to go since I saw Braveheart as a child: Scotland.

*Jonathan Thomas*

# CHAPTER TWENTY
## BORDERS

As an American, I don't often think about borders. I live very far away from the nearest international border with Canada and even further from Mexico. Each state has a border, and I live a few miles from several, but you never really notice much when you cross them. America is much the same place, wherever you go, with just a few variations. We have the same Wal-Marts and gas stations everywhere. Our borders are generally arbitrary and weren't really fought over (though my state Indiana did almost fight Michigan for access to Lake Michigan).

The borders between the countries on the island of Great Britain act much like the state borders in the USA do, but they have much more history surrounding them. Wales, for example, has been so integrated with England for so long its border - even when it's marked by Offa's Dyke, is practically invisible. The one that was much more fought over was the border between England and Scotland. It's moved countless times, but it's been in roughly the same place all throughout history. Even to the Romans, the wilds north of their border contained the disorderly, barbarian world of the Picts.

Since the Romans, the English have fought countless battles to control their whole island, much to the annoyance of the Scots. In recent years, there's been a lot of talk of this seemingly innocuous line on a map becoming a 'real' border again. Nationalism is strong in Scotland. Scotland has gained significant amounts of autonomy in recent years - in the 90s, its parliament was reconstituted and it was given back control over many of its internal affairs, and its First Minister is a respected leader throughout Britain.

Until this trip, I had never been to Scotland. For several reasons. Mostly because my heart lives in England. In the abstract, I've always wanted to go to Scotland, but getting there from the rest of Britain is quite a challenge, and there is already so much to see and do in England; it's hard to find more time and add more things to see. One of the reasons for our drive was so we would be able to see Scotland from the border to the sea, all of it. It would be a real treat. And in the process, I would fall in love with a whole other country. I didn't know that when we stopped off the motorway at the border crossing, where there is conveniently a parking area to take pictures at the massive border flag.

Over centuries, borders have often been tenuous things. They have defined national identity, determined settlements, and divvied up resources amongst peoples. The Anglo-Scottish border, since before recorded history, has divided two peoples from the Picts and the Britons to the Celts and Anglo-Saxons up to the Scottish and English. It is a long and sometimes bloody history that was not finalized until the 18th century, with often complicated laws affecting those caught in the middle.

The Celts first came to what is now Great Britain during the Iron Age, having been displaced by the expansion of the Roman Empire. The Romans would follow not more than a century afterwards, and most of Britain would end up divided into Roman Britain and Pictish tribal lands, eventually following the divide created by Hadrian's Wall in 122 AD. Twenty years later, the Antonine Wall would form the northernmost border of the Roman Empire in response to attacks from the Picts, who were descended from the Caledonian tribes that originally inhabited the region. These fortifications would mark the first borders between these lands. The area between them would form the basis for many later disputes and conflicts between the Scots and the English. As the Anglo-Saxons invaded and began to form the kingdoms that would eventually coalesce into a nation, the Celts resisted further advance, and the two sides eventually morphed into the kingdoms of England and Scotland.

There is a misconception that Hadrian's Wall formed the original border between England and Scotland, but it has always been firmly on the English side. The Antonine Wall only lasted 20 years before it was abandoned, and the Roman Empire relied on local tribes on the northern side of the wall to help repel invaders.

Border conflicts were fairly common during this period, with devastating results for those who lived in the lands caught in the crossfire. For lack of a better comparison, it was like the Wild West, a lawless area where the only enforcement was the sword and spear. People feared not only for their lives but their livelihoods as well, unable or unwilling to grow crops that would only be seized or devastated by opposing forces. In 1249,

King Henry III of England and King Alexander II of Scotland agreed to the creation of the March Law, which was designed to prosecute offenses committed by the forces or persons of one of the nations acting against the other. March Law was more often enforced during times of truce and virtually ignored by both countries when they were at war with one another. People who lived in the Marches along the border had mixed allegiances and towns or tribes switched sides depending on who was king.

  The town of Berwick-upon-Tweed is a border town that often felt the brunt of the conflict and switched sides several times until the English finally took control of it in 1482. The Wales and Berwick Act 1746 firmly established Berwick as being English (we did not stop in Berwick, we needed to get to Edinburgh for the timing of the rest of our trip to work).

  Following the death of Margaret, the daughter, and heir to the late King Alexander III of Scotland, King Edward I of England began slowly plotting to seize control of Scotland; following on a promise to marry Margaret to his son, the future King Edward II. England's invasion in 1296 kicked off the Scottish Wars of Independence that would rage in two distinct campaigns until the Treaty of Berwick in 1357. In the aftermath the counties between England and Scotland became known as the Debatable Lands, and conflicts here were almost invariably as local as they were national, with battles between neighbors also serving as fights between the two countries. Eventually, the dispute was settled between England and Scotland, with the French ambassador acting as an intermediary. The Scots Dike was then established in 1552, an official border with square terminal stones bearing the royal arms of England and Scotland, letting people know which side they were on. The border today largely follows this line. The modern Anglo-Scottish border is

96 miles long and stretches from just north of Berwick-upon-Tweed in the East and Gretna in the West.

Despite this issue being resolved, border raids, conflicts, and a sort of cold war between the nations, continued until after the death of Queen Elizabeth I. With the ascension of King James VI of Scotland to the English throne in 1603, the Union of the Crowns resolved any further border disputes. This peace endured until the English Civil Wars saw Scotland side with King Charles I, leading to further conflicts between Scotland and England led by Oliver Cromwell. The Restoration of King Charles II also restored the peace until King James II of England and VII of Scotland was deposed in the Glorious Revolution, at which point Jacobite uprisings continued until the Acts of Union 1707 finally ended the conflict between the two countries (save for a few more smaller Jacobite uprisings that failed).

Following the Acts of Union, Scotland lost its parliament, and its representatives went to the new Parliament for all of Great Britain in London at the Palace of Westminster. Border disputes ended, but Scotland's proud nationalism did not. While Scotland became a fully paid-up participant in the expanding British Empire, there was always a movement for Scotland to have its own voice and be its own country. Because of its small population, many Scots feel like they don't have an equal voice in the governance of the United Kingdom (5.4 million Scots versus 67.8 million English). Campaigning led to the reconstitution of the Scottish Parliament, but this was not enough for some people. The main political goal of the Scottish National Party, the main party in power, is an independent Scotland. In the last referendum, they failed to win a majority of the vote. That has not stopped them from trying to hold another vote though, in the wake of the Brexit referendum, the appetite for massive sea-changing referendums has dulled a bit.

While there is no border frontier, and passing from one country to the other is practically unnoticeable, you know you're crossing the border because Scotland has put up a massive flag and sign to let you know. There's a small lay-by at the exact spot of the border, where tourists like us can get out of our cars and take pictures in front of the big 'Welcome to Scotland' sign. We did our tourist duty and did so. We'd been in the car for several hours already, so it was nice to stretch our legs, and do the one leg in one country, one leg in the other, trick. Such a simple, peaceful, and mundane thing, crossing the border. In centuries past, it was not such a simple, peaceful thing. We're lucky that we live in such times that it's not a big deal.

After we crossed the border from England to Scotland, what surprised me most was how much like England it looked, at least at first. The Scottish and the English have been inhabiting the same island for thousands of years. For most of history, violently. Each country has its own unique landscapes and cultures. Yet they shared the commonality of trying to make this wet and somewhat inhospitable island home. So much so they've fought over the control of it for almost the entirety of their history. Becoming part of the same country - The United Kingdom - is only a recent development and the integrity of that Kingdom is at risk these days. I have no skin in the game, but I think the United Kingdom is better off united as long as the constituent countries are given a voice and feel like they have it.

As we approached Edinburgh, Scotland's stately and beautiful capital, the landscape began to change. It no longer looked like England. It looked like Scotland.

And it would for the rest of our trip.

*Jonathan Thomas*

# CHAPTER TWENTY-ONE

## Edinburgh

One of my biggest regrets from our grand adventure was that we did not give Edinburgh more than 24 hours. We just didn't have the time. But frankly, we simply did not plan enough time, it deserved more than we gave to it.

After we'd crossed the border into Scotland, it was not a long drive to Edinburgh. The most surprising thing about the drive was that it didn't quite feel like we were in a different country. Southern Scotland looked very much like Northern England. Endless green rolling hills. But don't tell the Scottish I said that!

And then, the landscape changes, and you see Edinburgh perched on a mountain, and you finally realize you are somewhere special. In keeping with our grand tradition of arriving in places at the wrong time, we promptly got stuck in traffic.

The fancy boutique hotel we'd booked didn't have a car park, so we had to park on the street. This was a problem. We drove around and around and could not find a spot to park near enough in walking distance to the hotel (we had to get all our bags there). Finally, we saw someone leave and found a spot not far from the hotel and then dragged our luggage along the cobbles.

The road in front of our hotel was a major, busy road, and it was all torn up and under construction. To be fair, our hotel was perfectly nice, but it was in the middle of a construction site, and I don't remember any kind of warning about this when we booked. After a long day exploring Alnwick and then crossing the border, we were quite ready for dinner and sleep.

The hotel was opposite a performance venue of some kind, and there were plenty of dining options there. When we saw there was a Nando's, well, that sorted it, didn't it? We had ourselves a nice cheeky Nando's and got to observe Edinburgh on a night out.

We were supposed to explore the city a bit - we had a list of things to tick off, but we just didn't have it in us. The problem with doing this drive in such a compressed amount of time (keeping in mind, by LeJog standards, we were going at a leisurely pace!) is that there's just not enough time to do everything you write down when you plan something like this.

In our case, we feel a lot of pressure - while we're enjoying ourselves, this is also our work. So we felt pressured to take one more picture, one more video, and get more notes for later articles. See just one more attraction. There's never enough time to see it all. But, since this trip, I've come to a comfortable realization that we can never actually see everything or do everything, nor can we meet the Internet's expectation to do so. So, we do our best. See what we can.

After all, not seeing something is just an excuse to come back. I don't expect my travels in Britain to ever be 'done.'

After a restful night's sleep, we woke up early and ready to get going. We had to wait, though, for our hotel to start serving breakfast. The problem was that since it was a boutique hotel and wine bar, it wasn't really set up for breakfast. They didn't serve hot breakfast, just some charcuteries and croissants. I left feeling very hungry. This one led to poor decisions down the road (like hitting a drive-through in desperation).

We loaded up the car to get moving, and it was a gloriously sunny morning, not a cloud in the sky. The plan was to visit the Royal Yacht Britannia and begin our drive through the Highlands. It felt wrong to just leave Edinburgh, there was clearly so much to see and do. Edinburgh's architecture was stately and beautiful, and there were plenty of cultural attractions to see.

We compromised with ourselves and decided to drive through central Edinburgh, taking random streets and just having a nose around. The highlight was a street busker playing bagpipes as we drove down one of the busy streets. Exactly what you'd expect to come across in the capital of Scotland.

Edinburgh is an interesting city. It has a weird position in Britain. It's a capital city, but it's not THE capital city. It's been recognized as Scotland's capital since the 1400s but, like other major cities in Britain, it's been around for almost a thousand years. The city's skyline is dominated by Edinburgh Castle, perched on a clifftop. It looms over the city, almost like a specter.

Long the symbol of power for the Kings and Queens of Scotland, Edinburgh Castle sits at the highest point of the city, a position that, at its construction, was both a great defensive position and forced others to look up to the crown. The reason for the castle's high position is that Castle Rock is the plug of a long-extinct volcano that hasn't been active for over 340 million years. It rises 130 meters (over 400 feet) above sea level, and its formation created three cliffs on the south, east, and west sides, ensuring protection as attackers could only take one path up the rock.

The first castle known to exist there was called The Castle of the Maidens and, according to legend, it was a shrine to nine maidens that included the Arthurian Morgan le Fay. The Picts and Scots reportedly built the castle in 1093 and, while we don't know much about its origins, we know that King Malcolm III was residing there when he died at the Battle of Alnwick in 1093. His wife, Queen Margaret (later, St. Margaret), was thought to have received the news of his death in what's known as St. Margaret's Chapel, the oldest existing part of the castle, though its architectural style indicates it was built during the reign of her youngest son, King David I, in the 12$^{th}$ century.

It was David who helped increase the prominence of the castle, holding the precursor to the Scottish Parliament there. The castle was given over to King Henry II after King William "the Lion's" capture for 12 years before the English gave it back, though Henry's great-grandson, King Edward I, laid siege to it in his attempt to claim the Scottish throne. During his time in control of Edinburgh Castle, Edward brought in the master builders who had worked on his Welsh castles to make improvements. It was later recaptured by the Scottish, then again by the English in the Second War for Scottish Independence, then recaptured again by the Scottish under William Douglass, who disguised themselves as merchants, then got their cart wedged in the gate while a surrounding force rushed inside the castle. This sort of back-and-forth siege of the castle would practically be the norm for hundreds of years to come, from the English attempt to capture Mary, Queen of Scots, to the Jacobite Uprising.

During all this time, however, major additions were made to the castle, including David's Tower, begun by King David II in 1370 and completed by his successor, King Robert II, less than 100 years later. At roughly 100 feet tall, it dominated the Edinburgh skyline for nearly 200 years until it was destroyed during the Lang Siege of 1573. While the castle changed hands, King James VI lived there until he was crowned King James I of England. The last British king to reside there was King Charles I before his coronation as King of Scotland. The last military action that the castle saw was during the Second Jacobite Rising of 1745.

From roughly that time onwards, the castle was used as a prison, military garrison, and armory. After a prison break in 1814, these uses largely ceased, and Edinburgh Castle began to take on more of a status as a national monument. In 1818, Sir Walter Scott discovered the Honours of Scotland, the oldest crown jewels in Britain, in a sealed room, believed lost since the Union in 1707. Despite a transfer in authority from the War Office to the Office of Works, a military garrison remained at the castle until 1923. Edinburgh Castle then became the responsibility of Scottish Heritage when the organization was formed in 1991. Since that time, it has become a Scheduled Ancient Monument (1993), a UNESCO World Heritage site (1995), and continues to be one of the biggest draws in Scotland.

Today, Edinburgh Castle's military and royal history is still on display, from the Scottish National War Memorial to the Scottish Crown Jewels discovered by Scott. It also hosts the annual Edinburgh Military Tattoo, a concert put on by military bands from all over the world. When not in use for a coronation, the castle provides the home of the Stone of Destiny (also known as the Stone of Scone or the Coronation Stone), which was returned to Scotland in 1996.

In the shadow of the castle, like most other cities in Britain that grew up around their respective castles, Edinburgh was a squalid and filthy place. By the first half of the 18$^{th}$ century, Edinburgh was described as one of Europe's most densely populated, overcrowded, and unsanitary towns. After the Jacobite Uprisings were put down, Edinburgh became an important city in Britain's growing empire. To match its developing importance, a massive undertaking of civil improvement was undertaken in honor of their 'new' Hanoverian Kings.

Vast areas of slums were cleared, and a 'new' city was built along Georgian design trends. Uncharacteristically, there were straight street grids with stately Georgian buildings (some of which were very tall). It was quite something to drive down and behold. From the 1770s onwards, the new Scottish middle classes gradually deserted the Old Town in favor of the more elegant residences of the New Town, a migration that changed the city's social character.

This redevelopment led to an explosion in knowledge called the Scottish Enlightenment. Geniuses like David Hume, Adam Smith, James Hutton, and Joseph Black were familiar figures in its streets. Edinburgh became a major intellectual center, earning it the nickname 'Athens of the North' because of its many neo-classical buildings and reputation for learning, recalling ancient Athens. Without Adam Smith, we wouldn't have The Wealth of Nations and some of the bedrock ideas of capitalism.

Edinburgh, like Glasgow nearby, was an important city of the Empire, supporting an aristocracy separate from the one in London but, for the most part, loyal to the British imperial project (if it could be called that, as it wasn't really a top-down type of project, it sort of developed randomly and suddenly there was an empire, but that's beyond the scope of this book).

It's a uniquely Scottish city. We will have to go back on the first opportunity and explore it more.

Press 2 then 0 then press PLAY
20

# CHAPTER TWENTY-TWO
## The Royal Yacht Britannia

We knew pretty early on that, when we visited Edinburgh, the one thing we had to see was the Royal Yacht Britannia. It's now the most popular tourist attraction in Scotland, and people quite enjoy poking around what used to be a very personal space for HM The Queen and the Royal Family. The yacht itself has a fascinating history - and its current status (and the desire to commission a new one) has become symbolic of Brexit Britain. When we visited, it was early in the day, and it was nice and sunny. The perfect day to explore an important ship.

The Royal Family travels in style wherever they go, and their conveyances include coaches, Rolls Royces, Land Rovers, a Sikorsky helicopter, a Royal train, an RAF Airbus, and even their own fabulous yacht—the Britannia. Colloquially known as the Royal Yacht Britannia, its official designation is Her Majesty's Yacht (HMY) Britannia (not HMS, these distinctions are important), and it has a long and storied history with the Royal Family. Britannia was in service from 1954 until 1997 and has not been replaced since it was retired. It was not, however, the first Royal Yacht.

The first Royal Yacht was the HMY Mary in 1660. She was the first ship of her kind in the Royal Navy and was constructed by the Dutch East India Company for King Charles II, a gift from the Dutch government celebrating the Restoration of the English throne after the English Civil Wars. Charles only used her for a year before he commissioned a faster ship and relegated the Mary to diplomatic voyages. Other royal yachts before the Britannia have included the William and Mary, the Royal George, the Royal Charlotte, and at least three iterations of the Victoria and Albert, amongst others. Several battleships have also been used to transport the Royal Family over the past century, with the last notable ship being the HMS Vanguard in 1947.

The Britannia's immediate predecessor was the Victoria & Albert III. It was built for Queen Victoria and was the first Royal Yacht not to be powered entirely by sails. Interestingly, Victoria never set foot on it as she didn't consider it stable, but her son, King Edward VII, made use of it during his reign.

The Britannia was the last ship in this proud tradition. Its construction was ordered on February 5, 1952, and the firm responsible was John Brown & Co. Ltd in Scotland (the Scottish connections of the ship dictate why its current home is now Edinburgh). Working from their shipyards in Clydebank, Dunbartonshire, the firm designed it to have three masts (a foremast, mainmast, and mizzenmast), with the aerials on the foremast and the mainmast on hinges so that the Britannia could go under bridges. The ship was capable of 12,000 horsepower and a speed of up to 22.5 knots. In case of another war, the ship was also designed to be converted into a hospital ship. The keel was laid down in June 1952, and it was the last fully riveted ship to have a smooth-painted hull. The ship's name was a closely guarded secret until Queen Elizabeth II launched the Britannia on April 16, 1953 (named for Britain's mythical national personification).

At the launch of Britannia, Empire wine was used to commission the ship rather than champagne as post-War Britain was still experiencing shortages, and champagne was deemed too extravagant for the occasion.

HMY Britannia's maiden voyage took place starting on April 14, 1954, transporting the very young Prince Charles and Princess Anne to meet their parents at the end of the Queen and Duke of Edinburgh's Commonwealth Tour. The Royal Family then embarked together for the first time on May 1, 1954. Of course, the Britannia wasn't for the sole use of Queen Elizabeth and Prince Phillip. Over its decades of service, the ship served sometimes as a love boat for newly minted Royal couples, ferrying them on their honeymoons beginning with Princess Margaret and Anthony Armstrong-Jones in 1960. It played host to a number of US Presidents, such as Dwight D. Eisenhower, Gerald Ford, and Bill Clinton.

Some of the royal touches on the ship include a grand staircase for greeting guests among them the likes of Prime Minister Winston Churchill, comedian Noel Coward, and South African President Nelson Mandela.

Besides shepherding the Royals all over the world, the Britannia had a number of roles unrelated to its original purpose. The Britannia sometimes traveled the globe as a representative for British business, pulling into ports and inviting CEOs from multiple nations to tour and experience its luxury for themselves. Known as 'Sea Days,' these voyages proved to be very profitable for the British government, and the Overseas Trade Board estimated that the Britannia made roughly £3 billion for the Exchequer between 1991 and 1995 alone. During the Civil War in Yemen in 1986, the Britannia was pressed into service as a rescue ship, evacuating British nationals and others. It was able to enter the country's waters without potentially causing an international incident due to its status as a non-combatant vessel.

Unfortunately, all good things come to an end. During the Conservative government of Prime Minister John Major, HMY Britannia determined that a refit to continue its use would cost £17 million. Major's government proposed commissioning a new Royal Yacht if needed in 1997, but the announcement so close to a general election may have been one of the factors in electing Tony Blair's New Labour government. The new government would not commit to a replacement during the first two years and ultimately opted not to replace the ship. Its last diplomatic voyage served to ferry Hong Kong's last governor, Chris Patten, and Prince Charles back to the United Kingdom following the transfer of the island to the Republic of China in 1997.

The Queen was not known to be overly emotional in person or in private, but when she was at the decommissioning ceremony, you could see her visibly cry. The Queen loved Britannia; it was her private home - her private bit of Britain - wherever they went around the globe. The crews catered to their every whim, and when they were at sea - sometimes for months at a time when on Royal Tours - it was a very private place. Some of her happiest memories were on board. When you tour the vessel, you get the impression that you're visiting a very personal place. There is no shortage of Royal Palaces in Britain, but they're rather grand affairs - that dwarf the human scale. The Royal Yacht was a functional Royal Palace-on-sea that reflected austerity in Britain, the era in which it was built. It's not grand - in fact, it's rather shabby - especially after years of sitting in a dock.

Now listed as part of the National Historic Fleet, meaning it has special protections and regulations for its continued maintenance, Britannia, as a visitor attraction, is moored in the historic Port of Leith in Edinburgh. It's a bit strange, it's attached to a shopping mall, which you have to walk through to get to the attraction. It is cared for by the Royal Yacht Britannia Trust, a registered charity whose sole purpose is to preserve the ship. There was some controversy in the siting of the ship - many believe that it should be located on the Clyde where she was built. But Edinburgh was considered the most likely place to attract the most tourists.

The ship is rather well preserved in aspic - much as it was when the Queen last used it. The rooms are rather large and impressive, considering they're on a small ship. Anyone who's been on another ship like the Queen Mary would be impressed. It is quite an intimate place to visit, like walking through a family home. It definitely feels more like a home than any of the publicly open Royal Palaces do. It takes a couple of hours to see everything on the ship though, if you're claustrophobic, you may not enjoy visiting the below deck areas where the crew worked. We quite liked our visit to the ship - which included a spot of 'proper' tea in the onsite café, which gives you views of the ship and the surrounding port. One cannot help but feel a faded sense of grandeur.

This is a feeling you often get throughout Britain but is perhaps something you notice only after repeated visits.

The fate of the Britannia has become another controversy in the department that is the endless war over Brexit. The current Conservative government, as of this writing, is proposing to commission a new Royal Yacht that would sail the seven seas again and become a symbol of the 'newly vibrant and free' post-Brexit Britain and drum up crucial business and free trade deals. A new symbol of Britain's soft power. The problem is that the idea is laughable in Britain's current cultural climate. The Royal Family has privately made it very clear they have no desire for another ship. The public has no desire to spend hundreds of millions of pounds on a white elephant ship in a time of pandemic-enforced austerity. The Royal Navy would rather not have to staff a ship of that size and run it.

Still, as an outside observer, and after having toured Britannia and gotten a sense of how things used to be for the Royal Family and Britain, one rather thinks that it might be kind of nice for a new Royal Yacht and a new generation of Royals to spread Britain's culture across the world. Still, I doubt they'll even build it. This idea is mooted every few years and dismissed in a news cycle or two. But it's not an idea that ever really goes away.

*Jonathan Thomas*

# CHAPTER TWENTY-THREE
## Driving To Inverness

The most frustrating invention that's ever been created is the average-speed camera. We do not really have these in the United States. They're absolutely diabolical. I'm not much of a speeder, but you have to hover as close to the speed limit as possible, or else your car rental company will get a speeding ticket, which they will happily bill to your credit card on file. Scotland, it seems, loves the idea of average-speed cameras because they were everywhere on our journey north. They were especially prevalent on the main stretch of road we took out of Edinburgh - the A9.

What does that mean, for you, a tourist driver on an epic journey from Land's End to John o'Groats?

It means that at no point on your journey through the most beautiful landscape you've ever seen will you go faster than 55 miles per hour.

This is both a good thing and a bad thing.

Scottish drivers understand this. They do not go over 55 mph through the Cairngorms National Park. Which means neither will you.

It's fair, really; you're forced to slow down. The roads can be treacherous when it's wet or windy - and it's Scotland, so that's most of the time. They've set the speech limit for a reason. So, best to just sit back and focus on your driving and not hover too close to the car in front of you.

Of course, Scotland does not have a monopoly on average-speed cameras. They're everywhere all over Britain, but I've never encountered more than I did on our drive through Scotland's glens and highlands.

One of the questions I get the most in the day-to-day running of Anglotopia is how you drive in Britain as an American. Everything is on the left. That must be hard.

The truth that a lot of tourist guides omit is that it's not really that hard. But then I've done it enough that it may seem easy to me. But really, it's not that hard. Once you're ON the road, driving on the left, you don't have many opportunities to go the wrong way. The flow of traffic simply won't let you. It can be rather disconcerting, speeding 70 miles per hour on the left side of the motorway. There is an element of 'this feels slightly wrong' - but you get used to it more with every mile you drive.

I've driven thousands of miles on British roads by this point, and quite a few on Irish roads as well, they drive on the left too. The hardest part is realizing the spacial coordinates of the opposite side of the car. We spend so much time driving on the right, that's how our brains think in traffic - and in safety. You know just about how much car there is to the right of you. You fully understand the spacial reasoning necessary. Driving on the left reverses that. Sometimes your brain forgets.

My brain has forgotten a few times - that's when I have an encounter with a curb (kerb in Britain) or a hedge on the side of the road. I will be the first to admit that I've been fined by my rental car company more than once for minor damage done to a car from not thinking fast enough about what is to the left of me, but thankfully, other than reversing into a fence post once (no damage, whew), I've never been in a serious accident driving in Britain.

In fact, I rather love driving in Britain. It's my favorite activity. The roads are very different, they are a different place. I especially love driving on narrow country lanes, as with each curve you often get a lovely view of the English countryside, which is where my soul truly lives. Even in the rain, there is nothing more pleasurable than barreling down a narrow country lane, with ClassicFM playing on the radio.

When we were planning the drive to Scotland, we knew it would be the most driving I've ever done in one trip, and I was neither nervous nor scared about it. I've driven in Britain dozens of times, I know what to expect.

But still, nothing can prepare you for driving on the incredible roads in Scotland.

Every road has a majestic landscape.

Every twist is something you've never seen before.

Every diversion is a change in weather.

Every mile is an adventure to somewhere magical.

When we left Edinburgh Castle, we headed for Inverness. I did not know what to expect on the way other than majestic beauty. I had no expectations of Inverness; I didn't know anything about it other than our hotel was across from the bridge that linked one loch to another. The further north we drove, the colder it got. Our Land Rover kept us warm and comfortable. This is why it was such a shock when we arrived in North Kessock and got out of the car, we were immediately freezing. Even though it was late September, it was like a cold November day in the Midwest of the USA. We didn't bring warm coats!

When we settled into our hotel room, up the stairs of a quaint Scottish pub, we were delighted to have a view of the loch and the bridge, but the old stone building was freezing cold. The room we were able to book only had twin beds, so we couldn't snuggle for warmth. We turned on the heater and still managed to freeze all night. We had a lovely meal in the hotel's restaurant. It seemed like THE place for the young locals to go for a nice date night out. We felt like the oldest people in the place - despite being only 35.

We did not linger in Inverness - we didn't have the time, and we knew that we would be coming back in a few days as that's where we'd catch the Caledonian Sleeper back to London. So, after a quick breakfast in the morning, we hit the road again and let our Land Rover warm us up.

*Jonathan Thomas*

# CHAPTER TWENTY-FOUR
## Loch Ness

Of course, we couldn't go on a drive through Scotland without stopping at a few fantasy castles. I do love a good castle. Our next one would be Urquhart Castle, perched on a cliff on the shores of beautiful Loch Ness. I was already all in for the castle, but really we wanted to see the most famous loch in Scotland as well. And maybe we'd spot the mythical Nessie (we did not).

We departed our cold hotel in Inverness and took a light diversion, this time not driving north but driving southwest so that we could take in the loch and see the castle. Loch Ness is massive (though not massive like, say, Lake Michigan, where we're from). But it also exists massively in the minds of Scots and the wider world because of the aforementioned Loch Ness monster, which is merely a vehicle to attract tourists to the place.

Loch Ness is a large freshwater lake located in the Scottish Highlands; it sort of cuts Scotland in half diagonally (the formation of Scotland's landscape is from deep geologic time: fun fact - the Scottish Highlands are technically the same mountain range that makes up Appalachia). The legend of the Loch Ness Monster, also known as Nessie, began in the 1930s and has since become one of the most famous and enduring myths in popular culture. The earliest known report of a monster in the loch dates back to the 7th century, but the modern legend of Nessie began in 1933 when a man named George Spicer claimed to have seen a "dragon or prehistoric animal" crossing the road near the loch. The story was picked up by the media, and soon many other people came forward with their own sightings and stories. Despite numerous searches and investigations, no conclusive evidence of the monster's existence has ever been found, but the legend of Nessie continues to be a popular topic of discussion and attracts many tourists to the area (which many suspect is by design).

You see the dedication to Nessie as you drive along the road that follows Loch Ness. Pretty much every tourist shop, restaurant, and cottage has some variation of Nessie as part of its marketing. All the gift shops are filled with Nessie tat. It's all rather amusing. You can choose to believe what you want but, if there is a Nessie, I highly doubt it was a pre-historic beast and probably more likely a big fish or whale that found its way inland.

We followed the coast road to Urquhart Castle, which is a lovely ruin that's firmly on the tourist trail in Scotland. The road was slow going, it's only two lanes, and with the volume of visitors, even in September, traffic slowly snaked along the loch. Which was fine, really, it just gave us more time to admire the incredible landscape. Growing up next to Lake Michigan my whole life, I was never really overawed by large bodies of water - but that may have simply been because Lake Michigan is so vast and the landscape around it so flat it's not that interesting. I'm not convinced I ever saw a 'proper' lake until I visited Cumbria earlier that year. The lochs in Scotland were something else entirely - vast but hemmed in by mountains. Primordial. Green. Filled with history. No, I didn't mind being stuck behind several coaches at all.

Urquhart Castle is a ruined medieval fortress located on the shores of Loch Ness. It could not sit more perfectly in the beautiful landscape that surrounds it. It's almost as if it was made to be endlessly photographed and painted. The castle has a long and complex history dating back to the 13th century. It is one of the most visited tourist destinations in Scotland, due to its striking location on the loch and its rich history.

Now a ruin, the castle was built in stages and went through multiple phases of construction and expansion over the centuries. The earliest known structure on the site was a fortification built in the 13th century by the Durwards, who were supporters of Scottish King Alexander II. The castle was originally called "Achadh na Casta" which means "Field of the Castle" in Gaelic.

In the 14th century the castle passed to the ownership of the Clan Grant, who expanded and strengthened the fortress, adding a great hall, a kitchen, and a drawbridge. During the Scottish Wars of Independence in the 14th century, the castle was occupied by the English and was later retaken by the Scots. In the 15th century the castle was granted to the Clan Fraser, who made further additions and improvements to the fortress, such as the addition of an upper courtyard, a guardhouse, and a prison tower. In the 16th century the castle was attacked and captured by the Earl of Argyll during a feud between the Frasers and the Campbells. The castle was later abandoned and fell into ruin. There is no shortage of ruined castles and family seats around Scotland (not to mention abandoned crofts, see chapter about the Highland Clearances).

In the 19th century the castle was purchased by the state, and restoration work was undertaken to stabilize the ruins and make them accessible to visitors. Today the ruined castle is open to the public and is a popular tourist destination judging by the number of coaches in the parking lot. We were impressed by the visiting experience. While it was rather expensive to get into the castle grounds, there's an informative visitors' center with a nice gift shop. You can then wander the castle ruins at your own leisure (but watch your step). You can explore the remains of the castle, including the great hall, the kitchen, and the prison tower, as well as take in the stunning views of Loch Ness from the castle walls. Really, the ruins are rather unremarkable by the standards of other ruins in Britain; what really sets Urquhart Castle apart are the views from it and its own position in the beautiful green landscape. I imagine you could take a picture every day of the castle, at different times, and you would never take the same picture twice. I like my landscapes like I like my British TV: dramatic. Loch Ness and Urquhart Castle deliver on both counts.

After leaving the castle, which was a slight diversion from the main route, we headed back north towards Inverness, then rejoined the A9 to begin our average-speed camera-monitored trip north. We crossed the impressive Kessock Bridge and marveled at the Moray Firth. That day, we had lovely weather. Rather than the torrential rain the day before, we had moderately sunny skies to see us north into the proper Scottish Highlands. And it was on this bit of the drive that The Fantasy started.

Bear with me here.

I've always dreamed of owning a cottage in Britain one day. But I always thought it would be in southern England - probably in Dorset or Wiltshire. The problem, though, is that real estate is at a premium in the South of England, more than it is in Northern England or in Northern Scotland. Curiosity couldn't help get the better of us, as we saw properties for sale along the road that followed the North Sea coast of Scotland; we looked them up online and were shocked at how affordable many of them seemed to be.

They could make the dream of owning a cottage achievable. And frankly, it didn't really matter whether I owned a cottage in Southern England, Northern England, Wales, or Scotland. I just wanted a cottage somewhere and, if we decided to make that Northern Scotland, it was probably something we could be more likely to achieve in a shorter time rather than waiting to save hundreds of thousands of pounds to buy a thatched cottage in Dorset.

So, as we drove north through Scotland, The Fantasy began. We'd find some unloved cottage (preferably an abandoned ruin) with a view of the North Sea. We would love it. We would restore life to it. It would become a home for us in Britain. We'd spend our days improving the house and the windswept property. We'd write every day. What better way to celebrate all things Britain than to do it daily from the Scottish Highlands by running Anglotopia from there?

We imagined all kinds of scenarios. This is what Jackie and I do when we go on long drives together. It's rather a fun exercise. The remoteness of Northern Scotland was precisely the appeal. It was a long way from everywhere else, and it would take a long time to get there. In the harsh winters, you may even be stuck in your cottage until the weather passes. Writing next to a wood fire while the wind and snow blow outside with views of the North Sea sounds like a kind of heaven only we could enjoy.

We must have seen hundreds of small cottages and abandoned cottages on our way north. We took a mental note of where the ones we liked the most were and, after the trip, we even went so far as to do some fact-finding to see who actually owned some of the abandoned ones. I should be clear, though, that the further away we got from 2018, the further away this idle fantasy has receded. It was nice to talk it out and imagine it all. After a forced four-year absence from Britain, I learned where my heart truly lies - in Dorset. So, that's going to have to be where my fantasy cottage will be one day.

It just has to be.

This day featured one of our longest stretches of driving on the entire trip. We traversed a big chunk of Scotland on our journey north. The landscape was empty, green, and beautiful. If I had to define a key feature of the drive that day it was passing over bridges on the various firths along the way. The road follows the water, as I'm sure the roads have always followed the waters in Scotland. There are interesting things in the firths. Oil extraction is a thriving industry in the North Sea, and the bounty of that, beyond oil, is that the expired rigs get towed into these sheltered waters to either be dismantled or refurbished for use elsewhere.

Oil is a declining industry in Scotland, but it will be providing important economic activity for decades to come. Even as the oil fields wind down, they will be decommissioning the oil rigs and equipment that made it all happen. Scottish Nationalists pin their hopes of independence on Scotland's oil bounty, but most analysts agree that it's not a long-term solution to fiscal independence. The world will have to move away from oil as climate change worsens. It's heartening to see

Scotland invest in alternative energy, and we saw the evidence on our drive through this interesting landscape. For every ship needed to service an oil rig, there are now ships to service wind farms, tidal barriers, and solar panels.

It was, perhaps, one of the most enjoyable days of driving I've ever experienced. And it was not over yet. Next stop, Dunrobin Castle.

# CHAPTER TWENTY-FIVE

## DUNROBIN CASTLE

To American eyes, Dunrobin Castle is a fairytale palace, right out of a Disney movie. Or Harry Potter. It's said that Hogwarts was modeled on its castigated towers and pale stonework. It's a magical place to visit, to continue the mixed metaphors. But one thing you will not find amongst the visitors to the place is many Scottish people. Dunrobin Castle is a symbol of a dark period in history. A period that turned the Scottish landscape into what it is today. The castle and the lands around it are a legacy of the Highland Clearances, an act of ethnic cleansing that had a major effect on the British landscape - as well as the settlement of the 'New World.'

One thing that stands out as you drive through the Scottish Highlands is their emptiness. A vast, unpeopled landscape. Filled with abandoned crofts (small-holding farms). Empty churches. In many places, the landscape has taken over.

But the Highlands were always empty. They were once filled with people. Filled with a vibrant, unique Highland culture that so much of the world seeks to identify with. A group of people in the Georgian and later Victorian eras looked upon this land and thought, forget the people; this land would be more valuable with sheep on it. And less troublesome politically.

In a stroke, the owners of Scotland's vast landholdings turned on their tenants and expelled them from their lands. When you listen to Scottish folk music, this is why so many of the songs sound so sad; it's baked into Scotland's history, imposed by outsiders, destroying a landscape and a way of life. Something that Scotland still struggles to restore to this day.

The Highland Clearances is a series of events that took place from roughly 1750 to 1860 and is arguably the most controversial and far-reaching event in Scottish history. It has been memorialized and cursed as a time when Highland lords and clan leaders turned their backs on their tenants for the purpose of lining their own pockets. However, the landlords also had their own reasons for reclaiming the land in order to pay massive debts. Whatever the reasons, the mass evictions of tenants resulted in a great increase in poverty and even death, to the extent that some Highlanders describe the Clearances as genocide (though that term is a 20th century invention).

As cities in Britain increased their populations at the beginning of the Industrial Revolution, their appetites increased as well, and the need for agricultural production became paramount. While the Lowlands of Scotland were mostly urbanized and industrial, the Highlands were more agricultural. The Highlands also still held largely to the clan-based system in which one family (headed by a chief) led other families that formed a larger agricultural collective or township. The chief leased the land to "tacksmen" who in turn rented it to the tenant farmers who themselves employed cottars to work it. It was very much a feudal system that had managed to last well into the 18th century. It was not an efficient system by any means in the age of more intensive farming spurred by the Industrial Revolution, and the landowners knew this. They wanted change. It didn't matter what the tenants wanted.

However, things changed after the Jacobite Rebellions and the failure of Charles Edward Stuart in 1745 to reclaim the throne of the United Kingdom. The new United Kingdom wanted to settle things once and for all and show who was truly in control of Scotland. The new 'British' government instituted new laws to penalize the Highland clans that had sided with the Stuarts and required them to pledge loyalty to the new Hanoverian monarchs or forfeit their ancient lands. Those who did not bend their knee were turned out of homes that they had owned for hundreds of years, and new landlords took over who weren't as interested in the welfare of the tenants. Additionally, amongst the new landlords and the old, the booming wool trade made many a lord realize that raising sheep was more profitable than crop farming in Northern Scotland's harsh climate and poor soils. Sheep didn't care about either and would thrive.

Landowners subsequently kicked the less-profitable farmers off their leased properties, burned their homes, and turned the land into grazing fields for sheep. You can see this in the landscape today. The Scottish Highlands are a beautiful and desirable place to live. And with property prices elsewhere in Britain being so expensive, you'd think naturally that people would want to live there - especially with the ability to work anywhere thanks to Broadband Internet. Yet, this area is still very empty. You will lose count of the abandoned cottages and churches, burned hundreds of years ago, that are still ruins. I often joke that you can't throw a rock in England without hitting an abbey or castle ruin. In Scotland, it's not as much of a joke - you can't throw a rock without hitting a former croft or church that was burned.

And this is where Dunrobin Castle and the Dukes of Sutherland come into the story.

Amongst the lords who changed the Scottish landscape, the Marquis of Stafford and his wife, the Duchess of Sutherland, were possibly the worst offenders of the Highland Clearances. They removed some 15,000 people from their farms between 1811 and 1821. Many of those rendered homeless, especially the old or infirm, died from starvation and exposure. They were brutal. And they benefited greatly from their brutality. The family still lives with this 'success' to this day. The family used their newfound wealth to build a stately home to show off their new status in Britain's 'new' aristocracy.

Perched on the coast in Sutherland County, Dunrobin Castle is no 'castle' - it's a proper stately home in the style of Downton Abbey or Brideshead Revisited. Don't let its castle-like exterior fool you, that's just a facade. The 19$^{th}$ century French style of architecture belies how far back the home's history goes. The roots of the Sutherland family at Dunrobin are deep, however.

The land on which Dunrobin sits was acquired by Hugh, Lord of Duffus, back in 1211 as a grant from King Malcolm I. Hugh was the son of the Flemish nobleman Freskin who had moved to Scotland under the reign of King David I and received a grant of lands from David in West Lothian and Moray. Freskin's son, William, was Hugh's father, and Hugh's own son William de Moravia became the first Earl of Sutherland sometime between 1230 and 1235. Freskin is considered the progenitor of both Clan Sutherland and Clan Murray. Clan Sutherland's motto is "Sans Peur" which means

"Without Fear."

Prior to the arrival of Hugh, historians think that an ancient fortress may have existed here. The original square keep was constructed sometime around 1275 and had six-foot walls, though not as much is known about it beyond this. The earliest part of the castle that exists today dates back to 1401 and has an iron yet (a latticed gate for defense). It is thought the castle earned its name from the 6th Earl of Sutherland, Robert de Moravia, as "dun" is the Scots word for "fort," and thus Dunrobin translates as "Robin's Fort."

In the 16th century, the earldom passed to the Gordon family when Elizabeth de Moravia married Adam Gordon, and the castle fell out of Sutherland's control. The next couple of hundred years made good use of Dunrobin's fortifications as the Sutherland family attempted at least twice to take the keep from the Gordons and, during the Jacobite Uprising, Scots loyal to Charles Edward Stuart attempted to take the castle from the family (who had changed their name from Gordon to Sutherland), though William Sutherland, the 17th Earl, managed to escape out the back door.

In the next century, the keep was expanded with a large house and a courtyard. The male line of the Sutherlands eventually failed in the 1800s and passed to the Leveson-Gower family through its marriage to Elizabeth Sutherland. George Leveson-Gower was the 1st Duke of Sutherland, and shortly after his death in 1833 his son changed Dunrobin Castle forever.

George and Elizabeth Leveson-Gower are controversial figures in Scottish history thanks to their participation in the Highland Clearances. Once they cleared the land, they set about building a stately home worthy of their growing wealth. So, what does one do? Why you hire one of the most famous architects of the day (Sir Charles Barry - who designed places like the Palace of Westminster and Highclere Castle) to build you one!

Beginning in 1835, Barry would completely redesign the home, turning it into a true stately home instead of the fortress it had been. The architect opted to build the new portions of Dunrobin in the Scottish Baronial Revival style. With 189 rooms, it was the largest manor home in the Northern Highlands. Barry also designed the gardens in a formal French style so that they extended down the back of the house almost to the sea (where the railway ran right up to the front gates, and they had a private railway station!)

The Sutherland family now had a grand home to match their grand ambitions. As for the people who used to live on their land and the other victims of the Highland Clearances? Many went off to Scotland's cities and became the backbone of Scotland's industrial heritage (notably in shipbuilding). Many others simply left Scotland forever, going to places like Nova Scotia in Canada and Newfoundland. Most notably for Americans, they came to America and became the first pioneers on the frontiers of Appalachia and the Midwest after the American Revolution. This rural Scottish life was recreated wherever the Scots found themselves. We live it today in the heritage of whisky making and in the language of the American South and Appalachia. These refugees even went as far as Australia and New Zealand.

While the Clearances had ended by the mid-19th century, the ability of landlords to remove the farmers from the land remained until Parliament passed the Crofters Holdings Act in 1886. The act effectively created legal rights to the land for the crofters, giving them the security of tenure so long as they lived and worked the land. They also had the right to pass the tenancy to their descendants and be paid for any improvements they made to the property. It would be nearly 100 years, though, before they would have the right to purchase that land.

While the Crofters Holdings Act effectively ended the Clearances in Scotland, the fallout remained. In addition to the suffering and death inflicted on the farmers, the clan system was effectively destroyed as many clan members spread to other parts of the United Kingdom, the United States, Canada, and elsewhere. In the years since, much of the lands that were cleared no longer hold sheep, farms, or much beyond the ruins of the townships. Some of these have been preserved as a memorial to a time gone by, while several have statues of those whose lives and way of life were lost. The Clearances also had a legacy in poetry, song, and literature, and the descendants of those affected still remember them with emotions that range from regret to anger. Ultimately, they serve as a reminder of what those in power can do if the rights of the people are not protected.

I didn't know any of this when I visited the castle on our trip. I just thought it was a beautiful and unique stately home, perfect for tourists to enjoy. I didn't learn about its dark history until I started researching this book after my return. I also learned that many 'nationalist' Scots see Dunrobin Castle as a symbol of their oppression by the British and the legacy of the Clearances. They would not visit the place for leisure, ever. I once came across a rather spirited thread on the Scotland Subreddit on Reddit.com, and quite a few people advocated burning the place down! Of course, it doesn't help that the Sutherlands built a statue lionizing their Duke who cleared the lands, which looms over the estate from the mountains above.

As you travel around Britain, in general, and learn

the true history of the places you visit, you begin to gain an understanding of the place beyond what the glossy guidebooks tell you. History is messy. Legacy is messy. It's something that Britain struggles to deal with to this day and you will regularly see arguments about the 'correct' interpretations of history in the British press. But that doesn't detract from the beauty of a place. The Scottish Highlands are beautiful now, as I'm sure they were 250 years ago. Dunrobin Castle is beautiful. Its gardens are sublime. Its history is dark but, as long as you acknowledge it, I don't think it's wrong to visit such a place.

The world we live in, especially in North America, was shaped by these Clearances; we would not be where we are without them. That doesn't make them a good thing. But it's important to understand these things, why they happened, and how they affected the people they happened to so that they don't happen again. It's perfectly all right to consider all of this while you enjoy tea and cake and then exit through the gift shop and continue on your journey.

Still in private hands, visiting the castle is like visiting a family's home. While it's a proper and popular attraction, it doesn't have the scale of a National Trust or English heritage property. When we visited, it was a quiet weekday, but the car park was still relatively full. It's a bit of a walk to the castle itself and, as you approach, you're presented with an impressive edifice, but this is not the view of the castle that's most famous, and it's not nearly as impressive as the proper one. No, that view is from the gardens.

When we entered the house, we were hit with a wall of warmth and, after being cold all day, it was glorious. There was a massive fire burning in the old stone fireplace in the entry way. It felt like a proper welcome to a Scottish castle. We purchased our admission and made our way through the house, it was a self-guided tour. While the place looks like a castle on the outside, it does not look or feel like a castle on the inside. No, it feels like a stately home (and hiss, like one you'd find in England). Room after room filled with marvelous and exquisite artifacts. Almost every room has a view of the North Sea or the gardens below. The rooms weren't crowded.

The Great Hall is the most impressive, with its ornate ceiling and intricate woodwork. The Drawing Room is another important space, with its stunning views of the gardens outside. The Library is home to an extensive collection of books and is a quiet and peaceful space for reading and study. I wanted to sit down and start working on this book immediately. The Dining Room looks like the perfect place for entertaining guests, with a long table and beautiful chandeliers. Finally, the Music Room is a wonderful space for performances and gatherings, with its grand piano and rich acoustics. Each of these rooms has its own faded aristocratic charm and contributes to the overall grandeur of Dunrobin Castle.

Before we existed the house, we stopped in the café and had a spot of lunch (and cake, mustn't forget the cake). We were grateful for a nice hot lunch, and a nice warm room to eat it in. Jackie decided that she would much rather stay warm and sent me on my way to explore the gardens on my own. I had a wander outside and the gardens were mightily impressive. The sun was shining but there was a cold breeze off the North Sea. I really wish I'd brought a proper coat on the trip. As I explored the gardens, I remembered to turn around, and there was the most famous view of the castle.

Perched on a cliff above me, it was a beautiful white stone fantasy of a place. Designed to look like what we think castles should look like (more akin to Walt Disney World, than actual reality). It did indeed look vaguely like Hogwarts and I could hear the Harry Potter theme playing in my head. Though to be fair, it doesn't take much for that famous John Williams' score to start playing in my head. I continued on, exploring the gardens, rather quickly, I should add, because I was cold. I saw a building at the edge of the garden and headed for that, thinking I'd be warm inside. When I got to the front door, there was a warning sign. Inside were taxidermies, and some people may find it uncomfortable. I'm not squeamish so I barreled in. It was warm inside but it was quite literally a horror show. Thousands upon thousands of animals, frozen in various poses. Some mounted on the walls, some freestanding. It was truly horrifying and disgusting.

Well, they did warn me.

I quickly exited back into the cold rather than spend one more minute amongst all those frozen, ghastly caricatures of animals.

At the edge of the gardens, there's a massive metal gate, and beyond the North Sea. Its waves roared in the wind. What I found interesting is that, while you walk through the gardens, you're shielded from the sound of the sea, and don't really hear it until you're right up next to it. By that point, I'd had enough of the gardens, and headed back to the castle, to find Jackie and make our exit through the gift shop.

As we resumed our journey up the Scottish coastline, we were excited because there would be another castle on our journey that day, and we'd be staying the night in it.

*Jonathan Thomas*

# CHAPTER TWENTY-SIX
## A Lament for Ackergill Castle

I slept in a castle once, and it's an experience Jackie and I, and no one, in fact, will ever have again at Ackergill Tower.

When we planned the trip, we wanted to finish off our drive in Scotland with a final hurrah. When I Googled hotels near John o'Groats, I came across Ackergill Tower. It was an old Scottish Castle perched on the North Sea Coast, and it had been turned into a swanky Scottish country hotel with a five-star restaurant. I booked a room immediately. Staying in a castle would be the perfect way to end our incredible drive.

We arrived on the grounds of the estate, it was late afternoon. On the drive up from Inverness we watched the landscape change from urban sprawl to remote countryside. Why the time we'd arrived in the county of Caithness, it was clear we were approaching the edge of the world. And after we drove down a private drive and came around a bend, there it was, the magnificent castle, glowing in the late afternoon golden sun. It was exactly like a castle in a fairytale (our second fairytale castle of the day). It's perched on the shore right next to the North Sea, which glistened blue like a million diamonds beyond in the sunlight. It is a beautiful medieval building with a central tower surrounded by lush green grounds. It was quite something to see.

I couldn't quite believe it was our hotel for the night. It seemed surreal.

All very Monarch of the Glen!

We parked our car in the front, next to a picturesquely placed green Land Rover Defender (I briefly pondered stealing it and shipping it home to the USA). It felt like a scene from Downton Abbey like we were up for a shooting weekend at a private residence. We checked in, and our bags disappeared as the staff collected them promptly. We didn't have a sea view, but we were in the main tower. We were led there by a helpful member of the staff. It was a precipitous staircase that wound up the tower, with stairs worn down by hundreds of years of history; it was like a fairytale, except it was real. We had to be sure to grab onto the ropes as it was narrow, steep, claustrophobic, and wonderful.

What a treat to stay in such a wonderful, special place.

When we got to our level, a massive wooden door was opened, and we were presented with our room. It was the former room of the lady of the house, and it had the most beautiful blue wallpaper, reminiscent of a William Morris design. The Lady of Ackergill studied bugs, butterflies, and flora and fauna, and the soft blue wallpaper was littered with the patterns of all of these beautiful creatures and plants. The room was massive by British hotel standards. We felt like we were high, on top of the world, from our room at the top of the castle. The view outside the window took in the estate below us, the large, green, manicured lawn and winding driveway. The only sound around us was the sea crashing on the rocks on the other side of the castle. It was a relatively calm day. We were lucky.

No one knows quite when the castle was built, but records began in the 1400s and 1500s. It's been a place that changed hands relatively frequently and was never held by one family for more than a few generations until the Dunbar family took ownership. The castle was cold and drafty for most of its history until it was turned into a stately home in the Victorian era. The changes, while still retaining the ancient parts of the castle, made the dwelling more comfortable for its occupants. Ackergill Castle became a place of aristocratic weekend parties and literary connections, despite its remote location at almost the far northwestern point in Scotland. Sadly, the Dunbar family eventually sold the castle and converted it into a hotel, but it wasn't just any hotel; it was a beautiful Scottish castle!

Just stepping into the foyer with the massive stone fireplace burning a welcoming fire, we felt like we were walking into history and were thrilled to add our own story to this special place. It felt luxurious to settle into our room, and we enjoyed the opportunity to relax in such stately surroundings as we sipped our tea and ate our biscuits that afternoon. I've never answered emails in a more wonderful place! We had booked ahead for dinner in the Great Hall, which was something to look forward to. It was a 'proper' restaurant with a fixed menu, chosen by the chef, incorporating what was local and fresh that day.

Before dinner, we had been invited down to the sitting rooms for drinks; this was like an episode of Downton Abbey. So, my wife and I did our best to dress smartly and made our way down the giant wooden staircase with its tartan carpet. We could sit in one of the sitting rooms amongst all the paintings and ornate furniture like it was our own home. We chose the sitting room that faced the coast, listening to the sea pounding the shore.

The waitstaff came in like we were the Lord and Lady of the manor, offering to bring a pre-dinner drink. We put our order in and took in the splendor of the room. In front of a grand window with a view of the sea was a beautiful old desk covered in books and papers, which looked like the perfect place to sit and write a book, while the sea lashed outside and a fire burned in the hearth. I knew we would have to come back and stay for a week, or a month, or a year and write the perfect book. The place was a fantasy, so we couldn't help but fantasize while we waited for dinner.

The castle had the most remarkable smell - a mix of old castle damp, old leather books, and the dust of hundreds of years of history - it smelled like history. Years after the trip, if you asked me what I missed about Britain most during our unplanned long absence, it was smells of places like this. Recently, when I visited Ireland for work for my day job, I had some extra time and visited an old church. As soon as I entered the nave, I smelled that old smell. The smell of the place. I was brought to tears, I missed it so much.

As we were waiting for dinner, sipping our drinks in our own sitting room, we heard a commotion out in the hall. We overheard the excitement; a hunting party returned with the news that they had successfully stalked a stag on the estate during their hunt. A bottle of Scotch was opened in celebration; this felt more like we had slipped through a wormhole in time, as if we were guests at a fine country house. The hunters and stalkers were still in their gear - tweed jackets, welly boots, and all celebrating. The whole scene felt like a work of fiction, not reality.

Precisely as we finished our drinks, we were escorted to our table. We walked into the historic hall, with its 30 foot tall stone ceiling and wood-paneled walls, in awe. We were seated in a stone nook near one of the large fireplaces, as the candles on our table were lit, as well as the candles surrounding our table that sat on ancient stone ledges. There was a warm fire burning just feet from our beautiful table. Dinner was a long affair, with multiple courses, and was the most opulent dinner we had on the entire trip. Sadly, I can't recall the precise menu, but I do remember plenty of game and locally sourced produce. We had perhaps one of the most romantic dinners of our life together under the ceiling of that great hall, tucked into our own little nook.

After dinner, we decided to take an evening drive through Wick to see what it was like, then down to the sea to hear the waves lapping on the shore. As Chicagoans, we are mostly landlocked, so to hear the sea is a treat (Lake Michigan has its own distinct freshwater sound, but the sea it is not). We retired back to our lovely room and settled in for a perfect night's sleep full of a delicious dinner and a feeling of being somewhere very special. Wick is a hard place with sturdy people. The town was practically deserted on a weeknight, save for roaming groups of youths trying to have a night out on the town in a place that wasn't really made for it. There's nothing particularly beautiful in Wick except for the harbor and the sea beyond. Like many places in Northern Scotland, it's economically depressed but trying to make itself better.

When we woke up the next morning, we knew our time was coming to an end with this magical spot; we had only booked in for one night. Before setting off for the day, we ventured over to the other restaurant on the property for breakfast, which was perfect in every way, complete with tartan tablecloths. The crowd at breakfast was rather interesting - quite a few Americans. And quite a few pilots. You see, Wick Airport is commonly the first stop when private planes make a transatlantic crossing (private as in single-engine planes). Pilots will stop off in Wick, refuel, stay the night, take in some history at the castle, have a nice breakfast, and then continue on their way (it can also be the last stop on the UK mainland for flights going the opposite way). We listened as one pilot explained their route excitedly to the couple he was going to be flying.

After breakfast, we took a short walk along the coast, and we were even more in awe from the shore looking back up at the castle. In that moment, we both vowed that we would be returning as guests to soak in more of the charm of the castle. After our walk, we checked out of the hotel, and our visit to Ackergill Castle was over. We looked back wistfully as we drove away, not ready to leave this special place. We both had a fantasy of coming back for a week in the middle of the winter when we'd have the place mostly to ourselves and write until we couldn't write anymore, punctuated by cups of tea and wistfully staring out at the sea.

Heaven.

It was not to be.

Shortly after our stay, we learned that our dream would never be realized. The castle, which was for sale while we were staying there, was sold to an American philanthropist practically in the cover of darkness. A planning permission application was quickly lodged to turn the castle from a hotel back into a private home. It was granted by the local council. The hotel was closed immediately, all the staff were laid off, and this luxury hotel in the North of Scotland was no more.

Only a memory for us, something we could never revisit. We were not only saddened by the news for us, but we had great concern for the amazing staff of the hotel, who were now out of a job. A huge blow to the struggling economy in Scotland's far north. It's heartbreaking that this beautiful place, along with the estate around it, is now closed to the public forever.

We can never go back, and neither can anyone else except the woman who bought the place, who has not ingratiated herself with the locals by making some of them lose their jobs. And that's a shame. Goodbye Ackergill Tower, you were lovely; thank you for sheltering us for an evening and letting us be part of your beautiful story. I wish we'd had more time.

# CHAPTER TWENTY-SEVEN
## JOHN O'GROATS

We departed Ackergill Tower after a nice hearty Scottish breakfast. We were not far from John o'Groats. In fact, it was only a 20 minute drive. We were bubbling with anticipation. And boy, was it a beautiful drive. The roadway hugs the coast most of the way. Endless views of the North Sea to one side. Endless views of green Scottish scrubland to the left of us. Occasionally there was a house or abandoned croft farm. There are hardly any trees up here, and the few there are permanently shaped by harsh winds that continually batter this far north end of the island of Great Britain. It almost felt like you were on the edge of the world and would fall off if you weren't careful.

We felt so very far away from London. It was almost 1,000 miles away. We were closer to Norway than we were to London. But it still felt very much like we were in Britain.

So, the question I've had for most of the journey is: what the heck is John o'Groats, and how did it become the endpoint of journeys across Britain. As always, there was a plan.

John o'Groats isn't even the northernmost point in Great Britain – no, that's Dunnet's Head, which is down the road. But this small Scottish village has become the nexus for anyone looking to complete the longest possible trip in the United Kingdom. More than just the endpoint on a map, John o'Groats is a charming place, a small village that retains its charm even with the flood of tourists who come for the view and a picture by the sign. But let's not mince words here; the village exists solely to serve the purposes of the route. It is, like its opposite at Land's End, a tourist trap.

And what would you know? It's owned by the same people!

Ferries still run out from John o'Groats to Burwick on the island of South Ronaldsay and back, and it's a ferry that started the village. John o'Groats derives its name from a Dutchman named Jan de Groot, who operated such a ferry from this point on the mainland to the Island of Orkney. King James IV of Scotland granted de Groot the ferry license in 1496, and de Groot started developing the area around the harbor as well as building himself a house, reportedly octagonal in shape. It's with this that the village first began to take root, though a number of local legends surround its founder.

One such local legend has it that the name of the village came about as a result of the silver coin that de Groot charged for his services, and so he reportedly became known as "o'Groats." While the term "groat" for this kind of coin predated the ferry service, the two became inseparable. Another legend has it that de Groot's octagonal house was built so that he could have an octagonal dining table that made every guest feel like the head of the table. The house was located not too far from where the John o'Groats Hotel stands today, and his gravestone (called the "John De Groat Stone") is located in the vestibule of Canisbay Kirk, just two short miles away.

There's a certain irony to the village that bills itself as the northernmost point of Great Britain. The truth is that Dunnet Head to the west extends roughly two miles further north, but John o'Groats has successfully cornered the reputation in Scotland. What's more, the furthest distance from Land's End is actually Duncansby Head, and the northernmost point in the British Isles is Muckle Flugga lighthouse just off the Island of Unst. Such is its dominion over this title, however, that the phrase "From Land's End to John o' Groats" is the British equivalent of the American phrase "from coast to coast."

As for the village itself, it's a fairly small place. It does not have a good reputation. Most guidebooks have classified it as a seedy tourist trap. One magazine gave the town a 'Carbuncle' award and declared it 'Scotland's Most Dismal Town' in 2010. Since then, though, there has been a significant development, with brand-new hotels and self-catering accommodations providing stunning views across the Orkney Islands. There's now even a Starbucks, which is a rather amusing thing to find at the northernmost point in Britain. When we browsed the shops were impressed. One was an Aladdin's cave that contained every kind of souvenir that someone who'd made it all the way there could possible want – from tartans and hats, to magnets and shortbread cookies.

Though spread out over the surrounding area, the total population is just 300 people, and its mostly devoted to the ferry and tourist trade. While there are cafés and shops, a distinction for the latter is that a number of the items for sale are hand-made and not the touristy bric-a-brac you find in most places. The Inn at John o' Groats is the place to stay when you're visiting. It faithfully carries on from the John o' Groats Hotel that was built here in 1875 and offers a number of cabins away from the main inn building that offers gorgeous views looking out to the sea. There's an extension of several structures that offer apartments and suites while adding a little bit of color to the seaside.

While John o'Groats has some beautiful landscapes, one thing is clear, people come here for the sign, which is modeled after the sign in Land's End (in fact, it was put there by the people who run the photo booth in Land's End). The original sign was constructed in 1964 to mark the "Journey's End" for visitors coming all the way from Land's End or just to see the edge of Great Britain. The man who installed it was also the owner of the John o'Groats Hotel at the time and would charge people to have their pictures taken with it.

As we approached, the flat landscape revealed the views of the Orkneys beyond, and we spotted the sign. It was covered in stickers from those who'd made the journey (the stickers have since been removed and the sign spruced up). There was a suitably large car park in front of it, which was mostly empty. However, there were a few camper vans. A few motorcycles as well. We parked the Land Rover and bundled up because the wind was FIERCE. It gave Chicago a run for its money. We quickly made our way to the sign and took pictures of each other. Another couple that arrived at the same time kindly took a picture of us together. And that was it.

"Well, we did it," I said to Jackie. A kiss was shared. We were elated.

"Tea?" Asked Jackie pointing to the Starbucks.

"Absolutely."

We quickly got out of the wind and into the shelter of the café.

"Looks, they have champagne to celebrate," pointed out Jackie.

"Well, it's warranted," I said.

When we tried to buy one, the barista said, "It's 10:30 am," meaning it was before licensing hours.

Oh well. I don't drink anyway.

So, we did the sensible thing and got cups of tea.

It felt like we'd achieved something immense, even though we hadn't driven that far, really. By American standards, I'd just driven from Chicago to Atlanta. But this was different. I'd driven the entire length of a country I loved very much. It seemed immense. It was immense. I saw so much of the nation that I'd been dying to see for my whole life. I can now say that I've been across all of Great Britain. I felt like I could say that I finally truly knew the country because I'd now, combined with the 20 years of travel previously, seen most of it. I could truly say that I'm an expert on all things British. We'd done it. It was a glorious and happy feeling to have accomplished something, no matter how small you might think it was.

I mean, it's not like we walked it or cycled it for charity or anything. We just did it for ourselves.

Which, at the end of the day, is a perfectly good reason to do anything.

But our journey was far from over.

# CHAPTER TWENTY-EIGHT
## The Queen Mum's House

What do you do when you lose the love of your life long before you were 'supposed' to? What do you do when you are an important figure in the Royal Family of your country but are no longer 'The Queen' and don't have a clearly defined role? Well, in the case of the Queen Mother, Elizabeth Bowes-Lyon, mother to the late Queen, you buy a castle on the remote northern coast of Scotland and spend the rest of your life dedicated to making it a home for yourself to your own taste and building new memories there.

That's exactly what she did.

When she found the Castle of Mey, it had been known as Barrogill Castle for a few years, and it was a ruin. The last residents were soldiers during World War II. The castle was in such a state that when she offered to buy it from the landowner, he practically gave it to her for free (though the fact she was

Queen Mother might have had something to do with that). It's not known how much she paid for it – some say it was £1, some say the owners just gave it to her, and others say she paid £100. The owners were going to abandon it anyway. It's the northernmost castle on the British mainland and not far from Dunnet Head, the northernmost point of Great Britain. You can't get further from the hustle and bustle of London on the British mainland!

The Queen Mother, like her husband George VI, was never meant to rule. But thanks to the selfish actions of George's brother Edward VIII, they were thrust onto the throne, having never prepared to be the reigning monarchs. But they both fulfilled the role with dignity and grace, guiding Britain through its darkest days during World War II. It was only fitting that the Queen Mother finally had a place she could relax and let down her hair after so many years of service (and who could have guessed she would live another 50 or so years beyond her husband!).

The locals were delighted that she bought the castle because it needed mains water and power, which would mean that they would also finally get mains water and power - something lacking on this remote northernmost post on the British mainland. The Queen Mother used her own money to renovate the castle and bring it up to modern standards, and it was a process that took nearly three years before it was a suitable place to stay.

In the darkest time in her life, she brought new life to the place.

The plan was for it to be a holiday home for her. She would not live there full-time. Her royal duties would mean that she could not live in such a remote place all of the time. So, she visited twice a year, like clockwork. She would come for four weeks in August and for two weeks in October. To be fair, those times meant she probably had the best weather for her visits!

The Royal Yacht, HMY Britannia, visited the castle several times, but the Royal Family stayed on the yacht as there wasn't room in the castle to accommodate them all. Princess Margaret hated the place, calling it 'mummy's drafty old castle.' When you tour the place, you can easily see why the rest of the family would just stay on the boat. It's compact. The Castle of Mey is not a grand home by 'stately home' standards. It was just enough to house the Queen Mother and her guests.

Only the hardiest of Royal Family fans will make the journey this far to see a place with royal connections, but they come in droves. It's very popular, and that popularity has kept the place in good condition since the Queen Mother died in 2002.

The house is now open for tours for a few months of the year. Tours are small, and you're guided around the place by locals. The tour feels like you're intruding on a very private space. This was the Queen's Mother's special, private place, and it has been left much as she kept it when she was alive. It is a time capsule of late 20$^{th}$ century Britain.

As I said, the castle is not a grand home, it's compact but classy, and it's a very intimate place to visit. It's a very neat experience to enter her personal space. Many artifacts from her life are present, including her clothes. The place reflects her personality. You'll notice small things like tattered rugs and curtains everywhere because she was frugal and would rather not replace them and keep using the old stuff. To respect that ethos, the house persevered in a sort of arrested decoration. It won't be improved upon, but it also won't be degraded as it is cared for.

My favorite room to see was the library, which was the Queen Mother's private sitting room in later life. It was where she was known to watch her favorite British comedies like Fawlty Towers and Dad's Army (there are videotapes stacked next to the old TV, ready to be played).

Before she died, she turned the house over to a trust and endowed it so that it could be opened to the public and cared for after she was gone. The house and the surrounding gardens continue to be managed by the trust. The castle is still used by the Royal Family occasionally and is available to rent out privately to the 'right sort of guests' (i.e. people who have staff in their employ).

Visitors can also stay on the grounds in new self-catering accommodation, which has the seal of approval from Prince Charles himself. When the tourists leave, you have the grounds of the castle to yourself, as the Queen Mother would have had.

The relatively new visitors' center provided a good spot for a lunch. It was here that we were introduced to the deliciousness that is a ham and cheese toastie, something we'd not had on our travels. Such a simple, but yummy and filling meal. It was a welcoming warm meal on such a cold day. The views out of the visitors' center were of the sea and the Orkneys. It felt like dining at the edge of the world. There was no more of Britain after this.

If you plan to visit yourself, we recommend trying to do so on a warm day... the wind off the North Sea is brutal (but the views across to the Orkneys are incredible!). The Walled Garden will be a nice respite from the wind. You cannot take pictures inside the house, which is a shame. They also work on a timed tour system, and they will not let you into the house before your allotted time, no matter the weather. Jackie was not amused to have to stand outside in the cold rain until they let us into the house. A picture of her in this moment is one of my favorite souvenirs of the entire trip.

It was the perfect place to visit after completing our journey across Britain at John o'Groats.

# CHAPTER TWENTY-NINE

## SCANDINAVIANS

The journey from Land's End to John o'Groats is over, but this trip is far from over. We were in the remotest part of Scotland and must get back to London to get our return flight back home. When we planned the trip, we intended to return the car at Inverness Airport and then take the Caledonian Sleeper train down to London. On paper, this seemed like a good plan. But it's those plans on paper that end up being bizarre adventures. The first mistake was thinking that Inverness was a bigger airport than it actually was.

We had dinner plans scheduled with a vendor for Anglotopia's imports business; he happened to be in the area and knew a good place to eat. We figured the sensible course of action would be for us to drop Jackie at the Inverness Train Station and store our bags for dinner, and then after we'd go and catch the train to London. As I dropped her off, the first disaster hit - our bag completely broke.

"Don't worry, I'll handle it," she said as she told me to get back in the car and return it at the airport - we didn't have much time.

I drove on, stopping at a petrol station to refill the tank - you always return a rental car with a full tank; otherwise, you can get hit with hefty fees. The Land Rover was a very, very fuel-hungry car. This would be the last major expense of the trip (it was well over $100 to fill that gas tank). I drove on and promptly got stuck in Inverness's rush hour traffic.

Eventually, I made it to the airport. And was rather alarmed. It was a very small airport. I knew it would be a smaller airport - but I didn't quite reckon it on being this small. I followed the signs to the Hertz rental car return and was led down rather narrow roads to a warehouse plopped in the middle of the Scottish countryside. It all seemed rather FAR from the airport. I couldn't SEE the airport from the rental return place. How was I supposed to get to the airport to catch a taxi?

I pulled up to the sleepy little rental return office, and there was only one other car there, a group of people dropping off a camper van. I parked the Landy, said my goodbyes to that magnificent vehicle, and went into the office to return the key. At first, the staff couldn't quite figure out why I was there (even though they should have known to expect me). I inquired as to how to get to the airport terminal for a taxi, and they said there would be a shuttle eventually.

Looking at my phone at the time, the clock was ticking away. I didn't want to be late for my dinner appointment.

After returning the key and concluding my business with Hertz, I stood outside waiting for the shuttle to the terminal. It was rather colder than I'd bargained for, and I didn't have a proper coat with me. Eventually, the shuttle arrived and me and the group of people who'd also dropped their van got on board. It was a five minute ride to the terminal.

Along the way, the driver spotted the Land Rover and positively purred.

"Oh, you don't see many of those returned up here. What a lovely vehicle," he said as he drove.

We were deposited in front of the airport terminal.

At least, I thought it was an airport terminal.

The sign said it was, but it was completely deserted, and there were no cars in the parking lot. There was a small glass and metal shelter with a sign that said taxi rank.

But there were no taxis.

There were no signs there would ever be a taxi.

So both me and the Scandinavians found ourselves standing there in the cold, expecting there to be taxis waiting.

It was an active airport, after all.

There was a phone in the shelter, with a small weather-beaten sign that said, 'if no taxis, call and we'll send one.' I dutifully called and ordered a taxi. They couldn't give an ETA.

I started chatting with the Scandinavians, who all looked rather weather-beaten themselves after camping in the Highlands for the last few days, and it became clear we were all going to the same place - the Inverness Railway Station. As it appeared there would only be one taxi coming, we all agreed to share one and split the cost.

They had thick accents, so I could only pick up every other word, but they told me about their trip. But they weren't flying out of Inverness because, apparently, no one actually did. They needed to get to the station and catch their train to Edinburgh, where they'd catch their budget flight back to Oslo.

We waited for that taxi for ages. I was cold. I was nervous about the dinner meeting (watching the clock). I'm not a very social person, and these Scandinavians were very gregarious and wanted to chat. And I knew it would be a long drive back to the train station.

Eventually, a taxi did show up. The driver didn't speak much English. None of us could really understand each other, but we managed to convince him to take us to the Inverness Railway Station. I took the front seat while the Scandinavians (three of them) crammed into the back with all their gear.

Then we promptly got stuck in what qualifies for rush hour in Inverness again.

It was one of the longest taxi rides in my life.

But we eventually made it back to the station, and I bid my new Scandinavian friends farewell. I paid the taxi fare and just asked that they pay the tip to the driver. They were very chuffed that I paid for it. I waved them on and walked into the station to find Jackie, rather weather-beaten herself from dealing with the luggage situation.

"All sorted, no worries," she said. Our luggage was safely stored, and we made it to our dinner meeting with time to spare. It was a fantastic meal, and a pleasure to meet our business associate in person. I tried Haggis for the first time. It was… interesting. I'm not in a hurry to have it again.

*Jonathan Thomas*

CALEDONIAN
SLEEPER

# CHAPTER THIRTY
## The Caledonian Sleeper

It sounds so romantic when you're planning a trip. Sleep on a train and arrive at your destination in the morning refreshed and ready to enjoy the day. The reality was... well, not quite that. My first experience on a sleeper train was not the greatest experience I'd hoped to have. It was certainly an experience. Would I do it again? Absolutely. Because how can you not? It's a train! It goes from London to Scotland or Scotland to London. And you sleep on it. It's a magical bit of place shifting that you don't have in a car. Someone else does the driving. And they do it very fast. Though the speed, I think, is what did me in.

It was something I always wanted to do and it seemed like the perfect way to end our trip. After dinner we waited in the train station for our time to check in onto the train. We could do it a few hours before departure so we could settle in.

It was very novel to us, this idea of going on a sleeper train. Having recently seen Murder on the Orient Express, I had quite a few romantic notions about our journey (without the murder). The harsh reality is that by the time we got into our private sleeping berth, we were both completely exhausted from our journey, and I was having a bout of an IBS flare-up.

This would not bode well for my first sleeper train journey.

Something almost lost upon most Americans is the joy of a good train journey. In the States, we're mostly used to taking planes or cars to get where we want to be, that we forget the simple pleasures of the railway. Amtrak is considered a joke - why would you take 48 hours to get from Chicago to Los Angeles when you could fly or drive? Over on the other side of the Atlantic, however, train journeys are much more common, and sleeper trains are making a comeback in the age of 'flight shaming' and climate change. The Caledonian Sleeper, though, is not new. It's been running from London to various destinations in Scotland since the late Victorian era (Britain's other sleeper train is the Cornish Riviera Sleeper from London to Penzance).

Sleeper cars have a history in the UK that goes back well over 100 years to the first used by the North British Railway for train journeys between Glasgow and King's Cross, London, in February 1873. Later that year, the Caledonian Railways added its own sleeper car that ran from Glasgow on Tuesdays, Thursdays, and Saturdays and from London on Mondays, Wednesdays, and Fridays. British Rail offered these services after the nationalization of the service in 1948. After 1995, it was run under British Rail's ScotRail division and remained part of ScotRail after the transition to a private corporation in 1997.

The overnight service that became known as the Caledonian Sleeper officially launched in 1996. It offered five options, each with a different name. The Night Caledonian ran to Glasgow, the Night Scotsman to Edinburgh, the Night Aberdonian to Aberdeen, the Royal Highlander to Inverness, and the West Highlander to Fort William. This arrangement continued until 2012, when the Scottish Government announced it was going to grant the Caledonian Sleeper a separate franchise. After a competitive bidding process involving Arriva, FirstGroup, and Serco, the latter won and began operating the Caledonian Sleeper starting in April 2015.

With a franchise that runs until 2029, Serco has done its best to honor the romantic history of the route's past while continuing to make the Caledonian Sleeper a strong competitor to airline travel that may seem more convenient. The Sleeper today runs two trains each week that go from Sunday afternoon to Saturday morning (but not on Saturday nights). The Highland Sleeper now runs three routes to Aberdeen, Inverness, and Fort William, while the Lowland Sleeper has two routes that run to Edinburgh Waverly Station and Glasgow Central Station. No matter the destination in Scotland, all Caledonian Sleeper lines operate on the West Coast Main Line with the terminus in Euston Station, London.

When we journeyed on the Sleeper, we had the unfortunate pleasure of experiencing the last days of the old rolling stock (carriages). Literally, a few weeks after our journey, they began running brand new shiny trains that completely changed the experience. So, really, we can't honestly review how the Sleeper is now - years later. Still, we were impressed by our private berth. It was certainly a novelty to us. We had our own room! On a train! Jackie took the top bunk, and I took the bottom.

We quickly got into our pajamas and snuggled into our bunks. We plugged in our various iDevices to charge. A purser appeared and took our order for breakfast - options were slim, but I ordered a 'bacon buttie' (a bacon sandwich). Our bunks were cozy and surprisingly comfortable. I was not feeling well, however, even before departure. Before departure, I had to make several trips to the toilet, which was fine, but it was unpleasant that you had to share it with the whole train, this would get more unpleasant as the night went on and more people used it. The Caledonian Sleeper is a very long train - with lots of carriages. And there's a reason for that.

The breakdown of the carriages is something quite fascinating. Since each route on both the Highland and Lowland Sleepers have different destinations, the trains will start out with 16 carriages for the Highland Sleeper and anywhere from 12 to 14 for the Lowland Sleeper. At their respective junctions in Scotland, the electric locomotive is detached from the carriages, and they're broken up into their respective routes, each pulled by a diesel locomotive. The carriages themselves are broken down into one of three categories: sleeper, seated carriage, and a club car (or lounge car). When ScotRail began running the service, they used the Mark 2 and Mark 3 carriages inherited from British Rail but, as of 2019, the Caledonian Sleeper uses new Mark 5 carriages, which offer state-of-the-art luxury.

And make no mistake, part of the reason you take the Caledonian Sleeper is for the overnight experience in one of its sleeper carriages. Travelers have one of three options when traveling on the Highland or Lowland Sleeper. The Classic Room is the cheapest option, with bunk beds, an in-room wash basin, and breakfast available for purchase. The next level up is the Club Room with twin or single bed options, breakfast included, an en-suite with a toilet and shower, and priority boarding and Club Car access. Lastly, the most luxurious option is the Caledonian Double, with a double bed and all of the amenities available to the other two. No matter what option a traveler chooses, they can expect WiFi, room service, and a complimentary sleep kit with Scottish toiletries. Additionally, you can opt for the seated carriage, which offers some toiletries as well as a sleep mask though, if you're like most people, sleeping in a bed is much preferable to the carriage seats.

    We departed on time and quickly got up to speed. It was a Tuesday, and I needed to do Anglotopia's newsletter before going to sleep (the six-hour delay meant it still wasn't late 'back home'). I attempted to do so on my laptop as the train lurched back and forth. But it became apparent very quickly that the wifi and the mobile signal I had simply were not going to be able to handle the work. The train was simply moving too fast to have a stable data connection. I'd have to do the newsletter the next day. So, I resolved to go to sleep, but my IBS did not cooperate. The rocking back and forth of the train did not help the pain in my bowel, and after a dozen or so trips to the loo (and it was filthy by then), I finally fell asleep. It was not a restful sleep, unfortunately. But I blame that on my chronic condition, not the train itself.

    When we awoke in the morning, we were just outside of London. It really did feel like we'd been teleported. It felt good to be in London, but it also felt like we'd missed out by sleeping through all the landscapes of England and Scotland on our journey. We were served breakfast on the train, which was frankly disappointing - one sad piece of back bacon in a bun that was way too big for it. Still, the tea helped wake us up. We dressed and repacked our bags, and when we stepped off the train, we were in Euston Station, ready for a day in London. We needed a real breakfast, a shower, and possibly a nap.

No, I didn't much like my experience on a British sleeper train. But I absolutely can't wait to do it again.

*Jonathan Thomas*

# CHAPTER THIRTY-ONE
## A Perfect Day in London

The sun was golden. The air had an autumnal chill. The city was not busy. Our favorite attractions were ours to enjoy. It was probably my 20$^{th}$ visit to London; I knew it as well as I knew my local city of Chicago. It was a second home to me. I knew exactly what I wanted to do during the one day I had in London. One perfect day. And I didn't know it would be the final day for almost five years. I'm so glad I spent that special final day in London.

The train deposited us at London's Euston Station at around 6 am. Neither of us had a particularly restful night's sleep, but we were at journey's end. We were in London. Our flight to Chicago left the next day in the morning. So, we had roughly 24 hours to enjoy everything London had to offer. We rushed around like drunk teenagers, not knowing that it would be our last time there in more days than we could count.

On several occasions, I have been asked what I would do in London if I only had a day to spend there. Usually, it's from a friend with a long layover. And it proves to be a very difficult question to answer. London always deserves more than a day. But what if you only had one day? That day we had just one. It was time to take my own advice. The problem we had with such an early arriving train was that it was too early to check into our hotel. We couldn't do that properly until the afternoon. But thankfully, we were able to drop our bags at the hotel, and they assured us we could have an early check-in.

First things first: we needed breakfast. The breakfast provided by the Caledonian sleeper was not adequate; one piece of bacon in a roll is not a hearty meal. We had a lovely breakfast at a little place down the street from our Soho hotel of choice - Hazlitt's; it came highly recommended by the concierge. It was called Balan's Soho Society Café, and they had a wonderfully delicious and indulgent breakfast. I want to emphasize the 'had' part of that sentence. Balan's did not survive the pandemic in 2020; it has since closed. The brand lives on elsewhere, but the place where we had that most wonderful of breakfasts on that perfect day in London is gone.

While eating breakfast we strategized how we wanted to spend our one last day, to do whatever we wanted before returning home to family and business responsibilities.

Let's live it up!

So, after our indulgent breakfast, we decided to walk through Chinatown, Leicester Square, and make our way to Trafalgar Square. Not only is this my favorite public space in London, but it's surrounded by great museums, most of which are free. We took a minute to say hello to Horatio Nelson and to see if there was a new work of art on the Fourth Plinth. Then we turned to our next stop - the National Gallery. This is my favorite art gallery in London simply because of the breadth of the collection. There is something to see for every art interest. But I'm mostly interested in the Turners and Constables. So, we made our way to the room where they're kept (you may recognize the room from Skyfall). I stopped to look at The Hay Wain, in fact, I sat down and admired it for quite some time. This is probably the most famous landscape painting of Britain and sums up the romanticized view of rural England the British have. I also looked at the Turners because I love Turner. Writing this now, almost five years later, it's heartbreaking to think that I would not see my favorite paintings for so long. I'm so very glad that we took our time that day.

Normally, after that, we'd have walked along the Thames down to the Palace of Westminster to say hello to Big Ben and maybe go for a ride on the London Eye. But since, at the time, Big Ben was covered in scaffolding, it was not a scene I needed to see right then (I'm happy to report that they finished the renovations and took down the scaffolding in 2022). Instead, I wanted to visit some bookstores.

I love the bookstores in London. I love bookstores in general. But British bookstores are special in that you will find a completely different selection of books than you would find in an American bookstore. It's an Anglophile's dream. You can find Britain's bestsellers and discover British authors you may never have heard of in the USA. Now, it's very, very hard to pick a favorite bookstore here. But since I only had that one day, I picked Hatchards, which is the oldest bookstore in London, dating back to 1797! The best word to describe this bookstore is 'stately.' It's very much the type of store you would expect the aristocracy to buy their books at during the height of British Imperialism. While it was bought up long ago by the bigger chain Waterstones, the store maintains its independent character and charm. I dream of one day being one of the authors invited to their Christmas book signing party.

I remember paying particular attention to the history and 'British' sections on the ground floor, then fanned out to explore the rest of the store. My interests usually gravitate towards non-fiction more than fiction. Many newer books will be signed by the authors, as many big-name authors will make a stop at Hatchards when their books come out. Inevitably, I will end up with more books in my hands that I will be able to fit into my luggage home. That's where the personal service Hatchards offers comes in handy. Depending on how many books you've bought (and how much you're willing to pay), they will gladly ship your books home for you. It's always a treat a few days after returning from London to receive a gift from yourself from Hatchards, usually wrapped in their signature brown paper. I also recommend joining their email list so you can order books from them when you return home. One of their pandemic projects was launching a proper online store, you can now order from them anytime.

By this point, after ogling some art and buying too many books, I was inevitably ready to eat some lunch. There are unlimited options in London. But since we were in London, not far from several locations, we opted for a cheeky Nando's. Nando's is not British in any way, but it's one of the most popular restaurants in Britain. This South African/Portuguese fusion restaurant specializes in one thing: jerk chicken. Well, two things, chicken and their delicious, amazing chips (that's fries for my fellow Americans). The chicken is so good, and the chips are out of this world. Be warned; this chicken is SPICY hot (and you can get it hotter if you dare).

After we ate lunch, we still had a big chunk of the day

left. We decided to venture over to Covent Garden, probably my second favorite place after Trafalgar Square. While it's easy to dismiss the place these days as just a fancy shopping mall and tourist trap, it's one of the most beautiful places in London that oozes history. I've watched it change quite a bit over the years - I remember when there wasn't an Apple Store! - but I always come back. The actual old market building is a marvel of architecture, and I love browsing the artisans at the Apple Market, which lovingly attempts to reproduce Covent Garden's old market credentials (and don't miss the Jubilee Market as well!).

Oh, and if you're peckish after walking here after lunch - I would definitely stop at Ben's Cookies. It's not hyperbole to sit here and type that these are the most amazing cookies on the planet. They're incredible. Don't buy one; buy a box because they make a great snack in the hotel for the rest of your trip. After this, we walked over to Long Acre and found the Muji store. Muji is a Japanese brand that has stores all over Britain. They make the best stationery and pens, and whenever I'm in London, I stop in to restock. I also buy their orange soap. I've been doing it since my first visit to London. Their mandarin orange soap smells lovely, you can't get it in the USA and, whenever I smell the soap back home, it reminds me of London.

All right, we'd done enough shopping. It was time for some more culture. We hopped on the Tube. Riding the Tube is a tourist attraction experience of its own. While it's not perfect and can get very hot in the summer, I just love the Tube. It's the quickest and cheapest way to get around central London other than walking. There's just something special about the smell of the Tube and the feeling of the wind on your face as the train approaches you on the platform.

By this point, we were exhausted, and we were notified

that our hotel room was ready. We decided to head back and get settled. We didn't really unpack since we were leaving the next day. But after several days in the car and a night train, both of us desperately needed a bath. Afterwards, it was time for a short afternoon nap. After that, I worked on the Anglotopia newsletter.

Now, for the most important question of the day. What were we going to do for dinner? We had to eat dinner early because we nabbed special theater tickets. So we booked a table at Burger & Lobster, a nice little modern chain in London that just has two things on the menu: hamburgers and lobster. As I love burgers and Jackie loves seafood, it's really the perfect restaurant (many will probably disagree with me and sneer that it's all just overpriced, well, we like it, so there!). After a delicious dinner celebrating the success of our trip, we went over to the Duke of York Theatre.

When we'd planned the trip, we'd managed to snag two tickets to the hottest show in town - Ian McKellan as King Lear. And since he's not getting any younger and we were both huge fans, we were very excited to end our trip by watching one of Britain's finest actors on stage and screen chew the scenery on stage. It was glorious. It's always rather exhilarating to share the same airspace with thespians you admire. The theatre experience is such an intimate one. While they perform the same show every night, it can vary in so many minor and beautiful ways. Each performance is unique. You're getting the actors at their best every time. It was a marvel to behold.

What a way to end our adventure. It was perfection.

The next morning, we got up early to catch our flight. The sun was just coming up as the taxi drove through West London to take us to Heathrow. I remember vividly the stately buildings of Kensington and Knightsbridge being bathed in the most beautiful golden sunlight. Everything went smoothly at the airport. We could not have asked for a better experience.

Since we started Anglotopia, when we'd leave Britain on our research trips, we'd be a little sad, but we always knew we'd be back, usually within the year. The business needed us to visit. It needed research, it needed content, it needed us to meet people. So, as we walked down the jetway to the plane that would take us home, I thought we'd be back in a few months. Maybe for my birthday the next February. We did not know it then but, when we departed Britain that day, it would be the last time we'd visit for 1,392 days, the longest stretch of time I would be out of Britain in 20 years. I didn't know any of the struggles the next four years would bring. I had no idea what was coming. All I knew was that we'd traveled the length of Britain, from top to bottom, and had an incredible adventure. The memories we made during those two weeks would carry me through the next four years of hardship.

# EPILOGUE
## 4 YEARS LATER
## 1,392 DAYS WITHOUT BRITAIN

I'm relaxing on a sofa in the sitting room of a cottage in the English countryside. I'm in silence. The patio doors are wide open, there's a cool July breeze, and it's raining. It's the most glorious rain I've ever experienced in my life because it took me four years to get back to this rain. To get back to England. To get back to an English cottage. To be sitting in the English countryside, hearing the rain. Hearing the birds. Hearing the rhythms of village life. I have finally, after 1,392 days, returned to the place I love most in the world: Shaftesbury, Dorset.

As my plane approached Heathrow, I had a window seat. When the clouds cleared and I saw the green patchwork of England's fields again and the British voice of the pilot informing of our descent into Heathrow, I cried with joy. I was finally returning. The landscape was different; it wasn't as green as I was used to. Many fields were golden yellow or dingy brown. England had just gone through the hottest weeks in its entire history, worsening a multi-year drought. But the land was recognizably England. It was recognizably home.

When I'd left England at the end of our drive from Land's End to John o'Groats, I did not know that it would be nearly four years before I would return. Running a business that was so intertwined with one's passion meant that I was able to travel to Britain at least once a year for over a decade. And then, four years, nothing. Four years can easily be summed up in two points: financial problems and a pandemic. There's really not much more to it than that.

I'd booked my return to Britain four times over the two years from 2020 to 2022. I'd booked and canceled it so many times that by the time I actually went, I didn't pay for anything because of all the credits and refunds we'd gotten over the years of disappointment. Every day during the first early days of COVID lockdowns, all I wanted was to be in England. To be locked down in a cottage in the English countryside.

I missed it so much that, in a period between lockdowns, I hired a local videographer to drive to Shaftesbury, put his 4K Camera on Gold Hill, and film life on the hill for an hour. Just so I could play it on a loop on the TV in my office so that it was like a window (you can still watch this video at https://anglotopia.tv). Whenever I was sad or depressed during those dark lockdown days, I'd pull up that video and listen to the birds and life on the hill. It was heavenly.

After I'd landed at Heathrow - and I had to restrain myself from getting on my knees and kissing the ground - I met up with my taxi driver. I'd been planning this moment for four years. I would take a taxi directly from Heathrow to Shaftesbury, Dorset. I had 48 hours to visit my most special place again. It was not nearly enough to get reacquainted, but it was all I had time for. Every minute would be a gift.

My driver was a friendly bloke from Shaftesbury, and thankfully he didn't talk my ear off for the whole two-hour drive. I slept on the plane, so I wasn't too jetlagged. How could I be? I was so unbelievably excited to be there. I knew the route to Shaftesbury by heart. If I'd been driving, I would not have needed Apple Maps' guidance. So, I sat back and enjoyed all the familiar scenes of home passing by.

There was bad traffic on the main road to Shaftesbury, so we diverted onto country lanes. They would take longer, but I could not think of anything better after a four year absence than driving through beautiful English villages in the golden July sunshine. I was there. I was home. The sun was shining. The sky was blue. The hedges were green and alive.

There was a big change on the cards for my trip to Shaftesbury. We'd said goodbye to our favorite self-catering cottage, Updown Cottage, in 2018 when the owners decided to put it up for sale. These are the friends that drove us around Cornwall at the beginning of the book. Well, then the pandemic hit, and they couldn't sell the cottage, so there was a little hope we could go back again. But four years is a long time and, eventually, it went back on the market, and it was back in private ownership before we could visit again. We would never get to stay there again.

Which meant I would have to find somewhere new to stay.

There are other self-catering cottages on Gold Hill, but I was not ready to stay there again. Too many memories. Too much sadness at the change. I could have stayed in our old B&B, The Retreat, which is still there. But I ended up renting the aptly named Gold Hill Cottage, which is located at the bottom of Gold Hill, across the street. It's a small little self-catering flat located behind a thatched cottage in an outbuilding. It's off the main road, with its own door. Very private.

And when you open the doors in the main sitting room, you get a stunning view of the Blackmore Vale, well, at least from the 'bottom' of the Blackmore Vale. The cottage was perfectly suited for my short trip. Just one bedroom and a shower and a kitchen area. The living room area was spacious and had a TV. But I was really there for the vibes.

After I'd showered off travel and had taken a short nap - the best nap I'd had in four years, thanks to the quiet stillness of Shaftesbury - I went out for food. I got to climb Gold Hill again and see my favorite English landscape again. It didn't matter that I got soaked in a surprise torrential rainstorm. After getting something to eat, I returned sodden to the cottage, changed again, opened the doors, and sat and listened to the rain while I ate. I love the rain so much. It rained hard, the clouds outside fast moving as they always do through the Blackmore Vale.

I'd waited four years for a moment like this, and it was absolutely delivering everything I wanted out of it. I was in a cottage in the English countryside. It was raining. It was one of life's perfect moments.

When the rain stopped, I decided to go for a walk.

I didn't travel 4,000 miles just to sit there and listen to the rain. The rain stopped, and the feel of Dorset had changed. It was late afternoon now, and the fast-moving clouds through the Blackmore Vale occasionally gave glimpses of a beautiful late afternoon sun. I put on my walking shoes, grabbed my camera (and my umbrella, just in case), and went out into the cool, moist air of a northern Dorset summer's evening for a stroll. For four years, this was all I wanted, to go for a walk in the English countryside, guided along public footpaths with the Ordnance Survey app. I didn't have a route planned or know where I was going; I just wanted to end up on top of Shaftesbury's hill so I could get a few groceries in town.

I saw on the OS app that there was a small copse nearby (English for woods); it was near the church in St James. So, I decided to walk over to the church and have a nose around. The air was still crisp and moist from the rain. I love old English buildings, and despite not being particularly religious, I also love its small old churches. I took far too many pictures of that beautiful old churchyard. I was just so happy to be there. I touched the stone walls, the aged stone cool and rough in my hand. It was so lovely to be touching an old building.

I left the churchyard and walked down the single-track country lane, occasionally dodging a fast-moving car (I don't know why I'm still surprised at how fast people drive down these narrow country lanes). I found the path to the copse and walked down it. All the bushes and weeds were soaking wet from the rain, all giving off a damp and rich aroma. Fresh Dorset air. It doesn't get fresher than this. There was a darkness ahead as the wood began.

Soon I found myself in a primordial place. It was dark and wet and muddy. I walked past the most beautiful gnarled old English Oak tree, its ancient branches reaching off into every direction. Its distinctive green leaves brightened the darkness when the sunlight slipped through the clouds. I tried to grow my own English Oaks during the pandemic to plant on my property in Indiana. It didn't work, they never sprouted.

I continued on through an open path outside the copse. It was filled with beautiful purple flowers. I'm bad at flora, I don't know what they were. I just know they smelt wonderful in the fresh rain. When I rejoined the country lane, I came across a large snail making its way across the street and took a picture for my kids. In that moment, I realized that I'd never actually seen a snail in real life. I stood there for a moment and marveled at it. What a remarkable little thing it was.

My path would take me now toward the highest point in Dorset. It went by Castle Hill, then up the hill beyond into another copse. I'd never been this way before, I was discovering something new. But I knew if I followed the map, I would find myself at the top of the hill that Shaftesbury sits on and have expansive views in many directions. As it was nearing sunset, I knew it would be worth the climb. So, climb I did until I came across a bench that had been in a situation to show off the view. I did not sit as it was soaked, but I did stop to admire the view.

Before me were the undulating hills leading to the Blackmore Vale, punctuated with trees and fields as far as the eye could see; a cottage in the Dorset vernacular sat perfectly in the landscape. The cloud cover created a peach aura over the whole scene as the sun was beginning to set. Everything was green and wet and glorious. I was so very happy to be there.

I could not have pictured this moment or that it would play out the way it did when I was driving from Land's End to John o' Groats four years previously. I was in bliss exploring the length and breadth of Britain. I took it completely for granted. I thought no one could ever take it away. Turns out, it could be taken away - and I would be the cause of it. That journey was one of those demarcation moments in life. There was before that trip, and there was after that trip. Nothing was the same anymore. Anglotopia was no longer my full-time job; in fact, I worked for someone else in a completely different industry. Jackie was working full-time for someone else. I don't know if Anglotopia will ever be my full-time job again. But I know it will always be my vocation.

I'd only been in Shaftesbury for a few hours, but I

found it pretty much the same as I'd left it in 2018. The town still looked the same. The landscape still looked the same. The ancient buildings I loved still looked the same. Melbury Hill still looked the same. There'd been superficial changes to the shops on the High Street, but the pub was still there. The church was still there. I was heartened to know that, even after such a long absence, so much would be the same. I didn't miss much. My four years gone was a blip in the 1,000 year history of the town. It got along fine without me. Oh, but what a treat to be back, even for a short time.

I made it to the top of the hill and found myself in the park to the south of the center of Shaftesbury. This is another favorite spot of mine. While I love the never-ending expanse of the Blackmore Vale, the views from the other side of the hill to the north are just as wonderful. You can see all the way to Wiltshire, and if you're lucky you can even make out King Alfred's Tower at Stourhead, which I could clearly see. I took far more pictures than I needed to. It was strange; I was there on vacation. This wasn't work. Every trip to England before the STOPPAGE had been a work trip, always seeking content. Now, I was a visitor on vacation, but I still couldn't help but capture everything.

As the sun was setting, I wanted to perfectly capture my first English sunset in four years. I wanted to preserve the moment. It took so much to be there again. The price was no longer measured in dollars. Every second in England again was a gift. But as I took those sunset pictures, picture after picture, I wanted to have proof of the promise I would make to myself, standing there in awe: it would not be four years before I visited this place again.

# Acknowledgments

Creation doesn't happen in a vacuum. First, I must thank J and S Colston, who were our sturdy guides during the Cornwall leg of our trip. Exploring Cornwall through the eyes of people who've spent their whole lives visiting it was an experience I'll always cherish. They knew what to see, how to get there, and how we could make the most of our experience. They took excellent care of us like we were family and were delightful and giving hosts. Simple thanks are not adequate enough!

I also need to thank John Rabon, a long-time writer for Anglotopia.net, who helped with research. He was instrumental in providing a lot of background research that went into the historical bits throughout this book. He was expertly skilled in taking my cryptic requests and returning interesting and thorough research.

I must also thank Anglotopia fans on social media and our website readers who followed us along on our End-to-End journey in 2018 for making the journey possible, and who have waited patiently for me to finally finish this book.

*End to End*

Printed in the USA
CPSIA information can be obtained
at www.ICGtesting.com
LVHW091334091223
765940LV00031B/1511/J